I0151380

The Panther Chronicles:
Part II
The Gold Tablets

The Panther Chronicles:
Part II
The Gold Tablets

Michael A. Kircher

Heckowee Press

The Panther Chronicles:
Part II
The Gold Tablets

ISBN 978-0-578-06824-4

Heckowee Press
Palmer, Alaska
Planet Earth

The Gold Tablets
Genesis

Whether led by an angel of the Lord or directed by the spinners of fate, the young man fell upon a large rock which appeared out of place amidst the moss and leaves in the woods. He slid the rock off to the side, revealing a smaller, flat stone covering a small makeshift stone vault. Removing this cover, he beheld a sight so out of place in the forest that it stunned his senses. A ray of sunlight percolating through an ancient oak flashed upon a series of small golden tablets, held together by a silver colored wire. He stood in awe as his eyes slowly resolved tiny letters and drawings of a nature very strange to him. He paused as he leaned forward, looked around to make sure he was alone. He reached for the treasure as his heart raced. As he examined the tablets, nineteen in number, he knew his life would be altered forever.

Chapter 1
News Update

Kirk Michaels established his reputation as a world-class photographer with his photo shoots inside Iran, Saudi Arabia and the Sudan. He was invited to lecture by his old alma mater, Kent State University in Ohio. On this sunny day, he and Lucy Graham relaxed in the lilac infused, warm spring air on a blue and green tartan blanket that Kirk bought for her in London to celebrate the safe return of her father. The MacDonald hunting colors of the blanket presaged the adventure that was soon to come. They were having an old-fashioned picnic on the south face of a gently rolling, bluegrass covered glacial moraine appropriately called 'Blanket Hill', overlooking the southern part of campus.

A faint ringing suddenly interrupted.

"Is that your cell phone or mine?" asked Lucy.

"Must be yours, I'm not carrying."

She quickly wiped the chicken grease off her hands, pulled the phone from the basket and answered. "It's Randall... Go ahead, Kirk's here, you're on speakerphone."

"While you guys are sitting in the sun having a picnic we've been hard at work."

"How do you know what were doing?" asked Lucy.

"I hacked into the GPS on your cell phone and pinpointed your position with Google Earth to Blanket Hill. Then I checked the weather in Kent. You guys haven't moved for an hour, so I assumed you were either having a picnic or ..."

"Never mind."

"And I suppose you're translating Sanskrit poetry with Nayana? Kirk said. "That hardly constitutes work, my friend."

"She's with me, but we've been spending our time, between snuggling, in the holographic chamber looking at the three dimensional photo projections of the carvings from the Panther Chamber."

"I didn't think we'd be able to keep you out of there, but why boor Nayana?"

"I'm not bored Kirk." said Nayana. "You have to see this stuff. I'm working with Randall translating the history of religion back three hundred thousand years. It's slow going but incredibly interesting."

"Kirk, we found something worth looking at while you're in the state. Remember our field trip to Serpent Mound in high school?" asked Randall.

"Yeh, that was fun. What about it?"

"I think it would be a great place to show Lucy." Randall said with an air of urgency.

"Oh, ah, okay." replied Kirk.

"I'll call back as you're on the way there; tomorrow?" Randall said in a rather firm tone. "Stop at the Kent UPS office. There's a package for you. Good luck and say hello to SCC."

"What was that all about?" asked Lucy. "It sounded rather mysterious."

"Randall is onto something, something big. SCC means secure channel or code. We use it as an abbreviation when we don't want anyone monitoring our conversations. Tomorrow we need to go to Serpent Mound. It's a beautiful drive. I think you'll find it interesting from an historical standpoint, since you did your undergraduate work in art history."

"Susan studied art history too, didn't she Kirk?"

"Yes. As a matter of fact she did some early research on Serpent Mound for a paper in high school."

"I knew you and Randall went to college together, but I didn't know you went to the same high school."

"We met in high school but he hung with a different group, the science nerds. We weren't really friends until we roomed together in college. I was into photography…the school paper and yearbook. He didn't really know Susan either. We just happened to be in the same class for the field trip."

"I see. I've heard of Serpent Mound but I don't know much about it."

"Serpent Mound is in Adams County, in Southern Ohio, near a little town called Pebbles. It's about a quarter mile long, three-foot high clay and soil snake-shaped structure. It's located on a plateau that rests on the edge of the site of an asteroid impact, very much like the

4

Yucatan Chicxulub impact sixty-five million years ago that sent those fragments into India. Remember the compass at the Jantar Mantar observatory in Jaipur that Randall studied? It was carved from those fragments."

"And the Black Stone in the Kaaba."

"Exactly. But the asteroid at Serpent Mound hit about two hundred and fifty million years ago. This was determined from geologic studies of the area. The plateau has a cryptoexplosive structure with faulted and folded sediments indicative of an asteroid impact. Somehow the early Americans sensed a special significance of the area and built burial mounds nearby, regarding the site as sacred. But the Serpent Mound itself predates these other structures. Recent carbon dating was inconclusive due to the possibility of site contamination. So nobody really knows how old the serpent itself is."

"Tell me more about Susan's research; if you don't mind?"

"I don't mind talking about her if you'll let me know if I overdo it."

"You can talk about her anytime you want sweetie. You've been good about listening to me go on about Jonathan. They were our lives and our loves. We'll catch up with them on the other side. But now we have each other. "

"Okay…her research. It was a paper for our high school Ohio History class. We took a field trip there and had to give our impressions. The reason I'm smiling is because she took it so seriously…spent a lot of time researching the area, calling scientists who did work there, reading obscure papers written about the area in the nineteenth century, etc. She must have put a hundred hours work into it. Got an easy 'A' of course. That inspired her dedication to her later undergraduate work in art history.

But Randall and I took one look at the aerial photographs of 'Serpent Mound' and co-authored a paper that attempted to prove the 'serpent' was actually a stylized sperm, impregnating a female ovum. We spent about fifteen minutes writing it. We both got 'A's. Our teacher said the concept was stupid, but original and well written."

"Sounds about right for you guys. Getting high marks for goobering together a piece of crap."

"Hey, whatever works. Anyhow, that about sums it up. Susan was pissed. She and I had been friends since grade school, but she refused to speak to me for about a month."

"I don't blame her. So her research was fairly exhaustive?"

"Yes. She even tied in early American migrations. She had the idea that the Lenni Lenape Indians migrated to Serpent Mound starting in the seventeen hundreds and established a colony there, when westward pressure from white settlers and other tribes forced them out of Pennsylvania.

"Who are the Lenni-Lenape?"

"You might have known of the Lenape as the 'Delaware'. They were called that because many lived along the Delaware River. The river was named after Lord de la Warr, Sir Thomas West, governor of Jamestown, Virginia in 1610."

"Yes, I've heard of the Delaware."

"Well Lenape means 'people'; Lenni-Lenape means 'original people'. Some believe the Lenape were the original tribe of the Algonquian speaking peoples. Although the term tribe is inaccurate. Technically they were organized in matrilineal clans with membership determined by their mother. Groups of clans were then called phratries by ethnographers. Each phratry had an animal sign: the three main divisions were the Unami, turtle; the Unalaxtako, turkey; and the Munsee, wolf. The Lenape were referred to as the 'Grandfathers' by other natives because the Lenape were here prior to other indigenous peoples. Because of their exalted status they were called upon to settle disputes among other groups.

The Lenape had a different concept of property rights than the arriving European settlers. The Lenape believed they were sharing their land with the white settlers rather than giving up title to the land. The immigrants, the 'illegal aliens', on the other hand, thought they were buying the lands.

In 1682, William Penn signed a treaty with the Lenape at the village of Shackamaxon, in what is now Pennsylvania. This treaty instituted a so-called 'chain of friendship', under which they could live in peace with white settlers. That worked fine until Penn died and his associates and descendants cheated the Lenape out of their land, ultimately driving them farther west. On their way the Lenape may have spent time at Serpent Mound because of its spiritual significance."

"But why is Randall so interested in Serpent Mound and the Lenape?"

"You got me. Let's see what's in that UPS package."

Chapter 2
Phone Home

Azure skies and bright sunshine easily convinced Kirk and Lucy to walk to town rather than drive. In the short stroll across the front campus they laughed at the show presented by the energetic, angry, and diminutive brown chipmunks chasing the much larger black squirrels out of their territory across the well-groomed turf. The view of the tall oak trees, the majestic elms, and the buckeye trees readying their blooms for a flowery display reminded the couple of the parks in London through which they often strolled, hand in hand.

Soon they arrived at the UPS Store in downtown Kent. They received the package from Randall and opened it, revealing an elongated, matte black quasi-plastic object. It was one inch thick with rounded edges and a slightly reflective surface encompassing about twenty percent of one of the larger flat surfaces. Kirk supposed this side to be up. The whole thing was about the size of an iPhone, but with no visible screen, buttons or openings, and significantly thicker and much heavier.

"I worked with various state of the art satellite phones in Africa, in the Sudan IDP camps, but I've never seen anything as peculiar as this." said Lucy.

"That's because this is a Harry Stratford product. Look at this note from Harry."

"Hope you are well Kirk. May this instrument keep you close to those who hold you in their hearts."

"How sweet." said Lucy. "This thing looks neat, but there is no keyboard. Where are the instructions?"

"They're on this little card. It just says, 'Speak and yea shall be heard'."

"You're kidding?"

"No. Look."

"Some kind of code?"

"Don't know. I don't see any buttons, anywhere. There are no openings. I don't know how you change the batteries or charge it. Let me try something."

As he held it up to his mouth, Kirk said. "Hello."

The device responded immediately and at the same volume. *"Hello Kirk. How may I help you?"*

"That's interesting. The whole case is a speaker phone." said Lucy. "It sounded like another person standing right next to us."

"It apparently uses a three dimensional acoustics projection. I've seen that emulated in a lab, but not adapted to small devices. That's pretty advanced. Let's try it again…Time and temperature?" asked Kirk.

"The time is now and your temperature is 98.7 degrees Fahrenheit, 36.9 Celsius." The device responded.

"How'd it know that?" asked Lucy.

"It must have biothermic sensors too. Okay. Let's try something else. 'How can I make a call?"

"Use your diaphragm to move air forcibly from your lungs across your vocal cords. Then modulate your vocal cords. For additional information log on to the Stratford Wiki."

"This is going to take longer than I thought."

"Sweetie." Lucy said. "I have a suggestion. Just use the KISS method."

"Lucy I'm trying to make a call on this contraption. We can play around later."

"No, no, no. I mean the K.I.S.S method; <u>K</u>eep <u>I</u>t <u>S</u>imple <u>S</u>tupid. Use simple commands."

"Oh. Okay." Kirk said as he pulled the device up to his mouth again. "Call Randall Thomas."

A small blue LED under the black reflective casing in the upper left hand corner started to blink repeatedly. It was visible through a previously unnoticed tiny plastic rod that penetrated the case to just below the surface.

Randall answered. "Hello Kirk. I see you got the instrument. How do you like it."

"It has potential, but I haven't completely figured out how to work it yet. I'm not quite used to satellite phones."

"It's much more than a satellite phone, as you'll find out. It's very intuitive. Just play with it a bit."

"How many numbers does it have in memory?"

"None. It accesses the database for that information. It has the contact information for the other devices of every member on the team. Everyone will get one. You can call Harry and Karl by just speaking their first names. If you say 'internet' you can connect to that at warp speed and verbally access data. Although you'll get more accurate information by calling the mainframe at our museum headquarters and logging in to the Stratford Wiki."

"Great. You say Karl Schmidt has one?"

"Yes. He's working closely with Harry now. Remember, he has a degree in Archaeology, and other useful skills. As I found out in Israel."

"What if I want to call a number other than the team?"

"It's programmed to access online phone directories; and some secret directories as well. You can call anyone on the planet directly, all you need to do is speak their title and/or full name, including the president of the United States, for example."

"Hmmm."

"Oh, oh. Don't even think about it Kirk. I'm not sure he's interested in your opinion."

"Hey. What makes you think I would call the president."

"I know you too well. You've gone several months without getting into trouble. Let's keep the trend going for awhile. Anyway, he has a secure Blackberry. You'll never get in; well, at least not anymore."

"What do you mean, Randall?" Kirk asked sternly.

"I, uh, sent him a text message once, untraceable of course. I kind of pretended I was a Chinese bank executive and we were calling one of the large loans we made to the U.S. I said we would take Alabama in lieu of payment. He responded that he liked the idea but there might be some objections in Congress. Anyhow, they increased security somehow."

"Probably just as well Randall. Alright. Back to business. How do we change the batteries on this thing?"

"Batteries? Kirk, that unit is powered on love. Keep the good feeling and you'll never run out of power."

"Right. Between Lucy and me we've already got enough wise guys here. Let me guess... nuclear?"

"Good guess! You'll run out of juice in fifty years, plus or minus. If it breaks open, walk quickly away. Just kidding. It has been drop tested from fifty feet high onto a concrete pad; completely waterproof and bulletproof. Also, as you might have already guessed, it automatically encrypts everything. No Bluetooth or pictures though; just 100 percent reliable communication anywhere on earth; in buildings, down holes, behind mountains. It doesn't matter. It's programmed to respond to the voices of anyone on the team. If anyone else tries to use it, the voltage multiplier circuit sends ten million volts at relatively low amperage through the unobtainium alloy case. Not enough to kill anyone, but strong enough to make them think twice about trying to use it again after they wake up. It recognizes voices very quickly, but to be safe I suggest you identify yourself before calling anyone, just to give it a second to process your voice. The software is still in beta testing."

"Now you tell me. It seems to be in speaker mode. How can I make a private call?"

"Just say 'private' next time you use it. It will then use that as a default until you say "speaker mode' again. Call us when you get to the sperm, I, uh, mean Serpent."

Chapter 3
Creation

Moving silently through space for eons, the five mile wide meteor eventually came upon a primitive, uninteresting little planet, third from its star, and in the early stages of its evolution. Captured by the planets' gravity, or guided there by the Greek goddess Iris, messenger from the heavens, it vaporized upon contact, creating impact features seven miles across, and reaching four thousand feet in depth. It deposited its Iridium signature, named after that same goddess, thus allowing modern scientists to confirm its origin and marvel at its effects.

The ancient features were sculpted by ploughing glaciers and were smoothed over by uncounted erosion cycles. Subsurface features masked through millennia by siliceous spicules, clays and sands deposited in shallow seas and hardened with age. And yet...someone sensed the anomaly, someone knew the hidden meaning of the site.

The Panther Chronicles Part II

Chapter 4
On The Road Again

K irk, I plotted a route to serpent mound with the GPS unit. We can take I-76 out of Kent to Akron, then 277 to 71 South toward Columbus, then…"

Four and a half hours later Kirk and Lucy headed northwest on state route 73, pulled up a steep hill on their right and entered the Serpent Mound Park.

"Well, that was a long drive but certainly worth it. I have to admit, spring in Ohio is beautiful." said Lucy as they pulled into the parking lot. "So that's Serpent Mound? It doesn't look like much from here."

"We'll get a better view from the observation deck."

"There are so many trees up here we can't get a good view of the surrounding countryside." Kirk said as they walked up the metal stairs to the elevated wooden deck. "But we're on a ridge at the southwest edge of the meteorite structure. It seems that the mound builders must have known that was here. It's way too much of a coincidence that they would randomly pick this spot."

"Well we've got a great view of the contours of the serpent from up here." said Lucy. "I must say, the extent of the excavation is impressive. Try to picture moving that much soil and clay with baskets and antlers for tools. This was definitely a community effort. The question is, what community?"

"Nobody knows for sure. Some researchers think the so-called Fort Ancient People built it when they occupied the area between 1000 and 1650 A.D. to time planting of their crops. Others say it's more ancient, built by an unknown tribe prior to the arrival of historic native American cultures."

"Fort Ancient People?" questioned Lucy.

"Yeah. We also learned about them in our history class. The Fort Ancient People occupied what is now Northern Kentucky, Parts of West Virginia and Southern Ohio. Not much is known about them. They relied on agriculture and subsistence hunting for food. Interestingly, they grew the 'three sisters', squash, corn and beans.

The beans fixed nitrogen in the soil for the corn, and climbed up the corn stalks as the corn grew. The squash grew along the ground and kept down weeds while the corn shielded it from the intense sun and protected it from the wind. Isn't that cool?"

"It is." replied Lucy. "Modern gardeners in the know still do that. My mother was a master gardener. She grew so many different vegetables in Saudi Arabia at our home. She had to keep them cooled down with a misting system."

"You know, Lucy, I think you can measure the common intelligence of a culture by the way they feed their people, and do so using sustainable techniques. By that scale the Fort Ancient People were very sophisticated. I guess they had to be to survive."

"Too bad some modern cultures haven't learned that lesson."

"Listen to this." said Kirk as he perused the brochure for information. "They say there may be great astronomical significance here. The head of the 'serpent' is aligned with the summer solstice sunset, and the coils are aligned with something or another, let me see…"

"Kirk, some people stretch the significance of everything. They see what they want. From my art studies I came to realize that our brains are hard-wired to recognize patterns; even those that aren't there. That's why some people think they see the face of Jesus in a piece of pizza. Others want to see an astronomical significance in all ancient structures. Most archaeologists are guilty of that one. Consider that some part of every structure on earth is aligned with some astronomical entity or event. For example, my foot is currently aligned with Uranus."

"Alright, smartass. But just for that remark you can buy your own lunch."

"Oh sweetie, if you buy lunch I'll take care of dessert…later."

"Deal! But before lunch I need to check in with Randall. I'm glad Harry provided this little satellite phone, or whatever it is. It's much easier to conduct secure conversations than with any cell phone."

"Well why don't you do that while I take pictures."

"Sounds good." Kirk replied as he held up the phone. "This is Kirk. 'Call Randall Thomas' ….Hello, Randall?"

"Kirk, this is Nayana, Randall is in the Holographic chamber. How are you guys?"

"Excellent. We're here at the Serpent Mound observation deck."

"Great. That's what Randall wanted to know. Hold on and I'll retrieve him."

"You know Lucy, Nayana is such a nice person, I'm glad Randall finally found his soulmate. They go together like…chicken and biscuits."

"Your such a smooth tongued devil. And always thinking about food eh?"

"Only when I'm awake. But I've been known to occasionally think of other things."

"Oh, like what?"

"Come closer and I'll….hold on."

"Kirk, are you secure?" asked Randall.

"I am now that I have Lucy with me."

"You know what I mean."

"Oh yes, there's no one else around, go ahead.

"Ever hear of the 'Walum Olum'?"

"Say what?"

"The 'Walum Olum' is a pictographic representation of the prehistory and creation myth of the Lenape. Some say the record extends back as far as forty thousand years. It loosely translates to mean 'Red Record'. It's considered by some to be a fake because some of the pictographs look like altered copies of Egyptian Hieroglyphics mixed in with Greek epigraphs. In addition, it encompasses old world creation myths, instead of the Native American archetypes. But what we've seen in the Holographic chamber here is apparently a copy of the Walum Olum pictographs similar to the one depicted by Daniel G. Brinton in his text "The Lenape and Their Legends" published in 1885."

"Well you built your Holographic chamber from the three dimensional holograms you took in the Panther chamber. So it's an exact depiction right?" asked Lucy.

"Of the Panther Chamber of course. But as you know, the original is no longer in the chamber. Our copy is incomplete due to deterioration over the centuries of the placeholders carved into the walls of the Chamber. It also varies in some important details from Brinton's analysis."

"How so?"

"The Walum Olum supposedly illustrates a creation myth and also depicts an epic migration to the new world by the Lenape ancestors. Nayana is still working on the translation of what we have. It's right up her alley as an expert on ancient epigraphy, but it's still slow going. She's running the pictographs through a software application she's designing specifically for the task. However there are some things that don't make sense. We'll give you the information as we get it. The whole process is complicated by the fact that there are apparently words in the Lenape tongue used to describe the pictographs. Modern Lenape doesn't always correspond to the ancient languages. The linguistics are extraordinarily difficult. We really need the original to perform an accurate analysis."

"So how could a copy of a migration to the American continent come to be in the Panther chamber beneath the Kaaba in Mecca?"

"Remember the Panther chamber is like a library, or an archive." replied Randall. "We believe that it's a kind of central repository of information about the Messengers from God who have appeared to guide mankind over the ages. That's what we speculated even before we went to Saudi Arabia."

"Like a modern day computer server, used to backup widespread information at a fixed location on hard disk drives. The desert environment in Saudi Arabia and the sacred structure of the Kaaba above, ensured preservation of the information, stored in the form of artifacts set into wall carving placeholders." said Kirk.

"Good analogy." said Randall. "Anyhow, in 1836, Constantine Samuel Rafinesque, a natural philosopher, published a translation of the Walum Olum based on wooden tablets or flattened sticks that he allegedly obtained from the estate of a Dr. Ward of Indiana. Dr. Ward was a Moravian missionary and physician who lived with the Lenape. He saved the life of the tribal historian, who allegedly gave him the wooden tablets in 1820. Rafinesque was considered a bit of an oddball, but he did have a unique command of languages, having studied over fifty before he was sixteen years old."

"Hmm." said Kirk. "A little strange and an intuitive language expert. Who does that remind you of Randall?"

"Hey! Mr. Michaels, you better not be referring to me." said Nyana in the background.

"Oops. Forgot you were on speaker phone."

"Getting back to the subject at hand." said Randall. "The wooden sticks were supposedly of birch bark, which makes sense since it was readily available.

However, the Walum Olum that was copied by Brinton in 1885 was still not from the original, as some researchers thought. It was itself a pencil tracing possibly made by Rafinesque as a backup of the painted wooden tablets that he acquired from Ward. These wooden tablets were purported to be a copy of the original migration/creation narrative that were supposedly written on gold plates or tablets. A Joseph Smith Jr. allegedly took these gold tablets from Cumora Hill Area in Manchester, New York, in 1827. Cumora Hill was thought to be a Drumlin, an elongated hill formed by the action of glaciers. But it either is, or the Lenape thought it was, a sacred structure formed by the earlier Mound Builders. So the Lenape may have hid the gold tablets there temporarily to safeguard them while they were in the area."

"And Smith found them. An interesting idea." said Kirk. "But what does that have to do with the Serpent Mound?"

"Smith couldn't produce the tablets later on when his story was questioned." replied Randall. "Smith's story was well known, so the local natives would definitely have heard of it. So we're hoping that the Lenape might have recovered them. Their migration route took them right past the Serpent. There may be some clues there as to the fate of the Gold tablets. If they had the tablets, the Lenape would have kept them close.

"In fact a village site was unearthed nearby belonging to the Fort Ancient culture." said Nyana. "So there is a precedence for habitation at the site. The Lenape could have adopted it as a home in the seventeen hundreds during their forced migration west, thinking the site would have afforded them some spiritual protection. Those who moved west later on, in the eighteen hundreds, took the tablets that they liberated from Smith and followed the same route."

"The migration scenario is consistent with what Susan's research indicated." said Kirk. "Randall, remember that paper she wrote."

"I do now!" said Randall laughing. "That's right. I remember she didn't appreciate our paper. And it was such a great piece. Well, her hypothesis may prove to be correct."

"That's not unusual." said Lucy. "Other tribes throughout the Americas would bury valuable materials to hide them from theft. Indeed, every culture in the world did so, otherwise there wouldn't be much of a field of archaeology, would there?"

"Thin gold tablets or lamellae were found in many Mediterranean area Greek and Italian graves." said Nyana. "The tablets from Italy's Thurii, Pelinna, and Hipponion graves and the Greek Island of Crete were inscribed with instructions for the deceased in the afterlife."

"Think they said, 'Walk into the light'?" asked Kirk sarcastically.

"Actually, Kirk," Nyana said with authority. "That's close. They referred to an ancient religious tradition that established the existence of the afterlife and explained, sometimes in great detail, the series of steps we would have to traverse, or the worlds we would have to progress through to achieve our ultimate spiritual level there. That's a recurring theme among many religions. For example, the Buddhists, Hindus, Zoaroastrians and the more recent Baha'is believe that when we die our souls traverse a series of spiritual worlds or conditions as we move toward perfection. That is, that we can advance spiritually even after death. Although some of the older religious beliefs have, over the centuries, morphed into the concept of reincarnation as a rebirth into a physical form rather than this advancement at the spiritual level."

"I used to hang out on occasion with some physicists who were studying quantum mechanics." said Randall. "After a few beers they started discussing some weird stuff that occurs at the quantum level; things that can't be explained by so-called traditional science. For example, they spoke of the possibility that the afterlife might be a transformation of our life energy, what we call our soul, into quantum form. We move into another dimension free from association with a physical body and become...light."

"Or it may already be in that form." continued Nyana. "Like a bird in a cage waiting to be set free, our souls may be held in an association with the body, here to learn what this world has to offer for knowledge and experience so the soul can grow. Have you had, on occasion, the feeling that you aren't part of the world.? That you're simply an observer?"

"Yes." said Randall. "Like the old science fiction movies where an alien comes to earth and takes over a human body, uses it to look around and learn about us, then discards it. I have had that feeling a couple of times; even when I was sober."

"The Greek and Italian gold tablets also speak of a goddess of the light." Continued Nyana. "This information was handed down orally from generation to generation until someone transcribed some of it onto individual tablets and placed it into the graves with the deceased. People may have even prepared their own tablets before they died. My own research indicates that the information they copied onto those Greek and Italian tablets is much older than postulated by most researchers, possibly by an order of magnitude."

"You're saying the religious information transcribed onto those tablets goes back more than the twenty-five hundred years age of the tablets?" asked Kirk skeptically.

"That's possible." replied Nyana. "The tablets date from historic times, the third century C.E. to the fifth century B.C.E. But I'm speculating that the oral religious directions for the afterlife written on the tablets may go back prior to the end of the last ice age, over twelve thousand years ago."

"How is that possible?" asked Kirk. "Weren't our ancestors a bunch of Cro-Magnons chucking spears at anything that moves? And how could that knowledge get from the old world to New Jersey, Pennsylvania, Ohio and the Lenape?"

"That's what we hope to find out." said Nyana. Remember, based upon the information in the Panther Chamber, we're studying religious tradition dating back over three hundred thousand years. We have to assume the ancients were much more evolved than is generally thought. They were intelligent enough to have benefited from contact with a messenger from God. In this case, perhaps a lady of light. Indeed, we're hypothesizing that the messengers were directly responsible for the advancement of humanity."

"That's back to the Punctuated Equilibrium Theory." replied Randall. "Humanity advances in spurts with long periods of stability in between. And the advance is caused by …God; sending His messengers to…"

"Kick us in the butt." said Kirk.

"What's the difference between that and the views of the hyper-Christian reactionary creationists that are trying to destroy critical reasoning in the name of God?" asked Randall critically.

"Lots." said Nyana. "Our teams' work is highly scientific in nature. Yet we all believe in a spiritual realm and a supreme being, and are curious as to His interactions with this material world. We have an open mind and seek the truth, although it is an excruciatingly slow and convoluted process. Our scientific minds aren't preconditioned by propaganda to believe something, then ignore or try to suppress everything that doesn't fit our preconception. We'll seek out the truth and let the chips fall where they may and let other people draw their own conclusions. That's the difference between inquisitive and an Inquisition."

"Touche`." replied Lucy. "If Spiritual beings, let's say, energized and advanced societies, then that may well be why Cro-Magnon survived to become us, while Neanderthals slowly died out. That is, Neanderthals, for some reason, weren't visited, affected or energized by a prophet."

"Either that or they didn't heed the advice of the spiritual Energizer Bunny." replied Randall.

"But Kirk." said Lucy. Getting back to our ancestors. You're a damn good photo journalist, but you need to study prehistory a little more, especially from an anthropologic standpoint. The Cro-Magnon type of Homo sapien was highly advanced. Today they're even referred to as Early Modern Humans. They built homes, cared for each other, farmed, and had rituals for burying their dead. I've studied their artwork. It's very sophisticated. I was amazed just by their use of mineral dyes in paintings and fabrics. They made instruments and played music. They were also excellent weavers. From the standpoint of our current focus, they're also genetically linked to American natives."

"All of my research over the decades has also led me to believe that the ancients were much more advanced than we thought." added Nyana. "Someone even suggested that you could take an Early Modern Human from a hundred thousand years ago and send him to school, through college, and he would come out just like us."

"He couldn't afford the tuition." said Kirk.

"He could always apply for one of those Cro-Magnon internships." said Randall. "I knew a guy who…"

"Ok wise guys." interrupted Lucy. "The point is, if you stand back and just do a general overview of what we know about them, you might conclude that they lived like a highly advanced culture that was devastated by a catastrophic event. Indeed, if we had a runaway climate change, say a very fast global warming scenario, what was left of our civilization might end up resembling that of the Cro-Magnons. Think about it. If we abandoned our cities as the result of an environmental crisis, they would disappear completely in about a hundred years."

"Or in an instant if they were nuked." replied Kirk. "I wonder how long it would take for future generations to regress to dispersed tribal status and forget about us after some sort of catastrophe?"

"Regress to tribal status?" asked Lucy. The whole world is currently operating in tribal status. We can cite as examples the tribes in Africa that take turns killing each other, or the various religious tribes in all countries, or the inner city gangs. And if you really want a large scale example of tribal interaction, just visit the United Nations during a meeting of the General Assembly. Or follow a presidential election in the United States."

Chapter 5
What is...Was.

The 36 inch drill bit cut into the earth on the northern slope of the continent. It passed quickly through the few tens of feet of unconsolidated top sediments. This top section of hole was then cased off at 150 feet using 30 inch diameter, 2 inch thick steel pipe. A 24 inch bit substituted on the drill string, allowed the driller to continue rapidly through most of the 1000 foot thick permafrost, a permanently frozen formation. A 20 inch, 1 1/4' thick steel casing pipe was cemented in place just above the base of the permafrost. "Keep everyone alert." The driller said as drilling resumed with a 17.5 inch bit. Soon after they drilled out the cement at the casing base, they pierced through the final section of permafrost into the underlying methane hydrate bearing formation.

Methane hydrate consists of methane molecules surrounded by a cage of frozen water molecules. It's a very concentrated form of the gas. When the ice melts, the gas is released. Pressure maintained in a gas well by the heavy drilling fluid contains the gas. Reduction in pressure can result in a rapid and catastrophic release of gas.

A massive pump circulated the drilling fluid that maintained proper hydrostatic pressure in the well annulus, the area in the hole outside of the drill pipe. This heavy fluid prevented the well from blowing out. Only one pump was needed to maintain circulation of this critical fluid, but the driller ordered both run for extra safety. There was virtually no chance that both pumps could fail simultaneously.

However, human error once again precipitated a series of events whose outcome would alter the course of history. The novice drilling engineer, on duty in the pump room, activated the number two pump too quickly. The ensuing pressure surge caused a formation fracture in the wellbore just below the last casing depth at the methane bearing formation. This was the weakest spot in the well. This resulted in a loss of circulation of the drilling fluid as it flowed into this widening fracture. The mud engineer, following standard operating procedure, quickly added water and nutplug to the hydraulic fluid to help reduce the pressure in the borehole and plug the fractured zone. This reduced the fluid loss to the fractured formation, but also reduced the pressure at the bottom of the hole. Due to lack of experience drilling through such formations, the crew was unfamiliar with methane hydrate containment procedures.

The drilling fluid circulating down the pipe and through the annulus warmed the newly drilled methane hydrate formation. Along with the pressure drop, this liberated the gas and allowed it to flow swiftly into the well. As the gas bubbles consolidated, they formed a huge, deadly bubble. Following the basic laws of physics, as the bubble rose towards the surface, the outside pressure dropped precipitously. The bubble expanding into a monstrous growth, further reducing the pressure of the hole and allowing another massive influx of gas from downhole. This process continued until it reached catastrophic proportions.

Despite intensive efforts on the part of the crew, the well had sustained a crushing blowout resulting in a terminally fractured methane hydrate formation. Widening cracks and cascading damage to the other wells drilled directionally from this one pad reached out to five miles in all directions in this gas production field.

Hundreds of production wells serving the hydrocarbon demands of this highly technologically advanced worldwide civilization suddenly mutated into this multi-legged chimera. Over the course of a single month these wells released a trillion cubic meters of methane into a complacent and unsuspecting world, and continued to do so until the pressure eventually equalized.

Most of this massive gas release eventually oxidized into carbon dioxide, but as it did, it completed the carbon saturation of the biosphere and oceans; a process well under way for some time.

Three years later a massive earthquake occurred in the outer continental shelf off the coast of what is now Central America. This caused an undersea landslide that exposed a submarine hydrate sediment, reducing pressure to the formation and initiating another massive release of methane. This was referred to as the ten-twenty event, named after the ten to the twentieth power, cubic meters of methane estimated to have been released. Unlike the previous oilfield emission, this was not absorbed into the already saturated biosphere. The ten-twenty quickly migrated into the upper atmosphere. Since methane is twenty times more potent in producing greenhouse warming as carbon dioxide, this triggered a runaway greenhouse effect, a tipping point, that rapidly warmed the planet.

Subsequently, as the polar and Greenland ice sheets melted, they sent fresh water into the oceans. Rising temperatures caused rainfall to increase dramatically. As a result, the salinity in the northern Atlantic waters decreased rapidly. The Gulf Stream, or the thermohaline conveyor system that supplied warmth to Northern Europe, stopped. This reduced the heat from the equatorial regions to the higher latitudes and triggered a sudden cooling in those regions, paradoxically initiating another ice age which encompassed the north. Twenty years later the population of the planet had been reduced by 95%, first by massive coastal flooding and famine caused by worldwide crop failures, and then by extraordinarily cold weather in the heavily populated northern latitudes. In effect, the carrying capacity of the planet collapsed. Wars for remaining resources increased, power systems failed and technology disintegrated. The last sparks of communication finally ceased among the tribal entities remaining. History lapsed into legend, and legend into myth …twenty-five thousand years before the present.

Over a period of thousands of years the planet slowly warmed and the climate once again stabilized. The isolated tribes increased their numbers with the advent of this more benign climate. Long unused ancestral languages were remembered and reintegrated into the current vernacular, passed on in the shadows of history by shamans and elders. Civilizations were rebuilt and trade prospered.

And as the last ice sheets retreated twelve thousand years ago, the tribes began to move into new territory, spurred on by exigencies of wars and natural disasters.

Chapter 6
Renewal

"O.K." said Randall. "Let's look at what we have for now. The Lenape ancestors migrated to this country from some unknown area. They may have somehow been familiar with the gold leaf tablets used in Greek graves. We're hoping that some spiritual tribal leader kept their chronology on similar tablets. Gold tablets are water and acid proof and show no deterioration with handling. They were easily engraved and difficult to alter the symbols without damaging the material. As a backup, someone could have transcribed the pictographs from gold tablets onto wood in the new world. That could be the set of tablets given to Ward and secured and copied by Rafinesque. They were subsequently lost when the extensive collections of Rafinesque were discarded after his death.

In addition, some biblical scholars predicted the return of Jesus Christ for this time. This was referred to as the period of a 'Great Awakening', an age of considerable religious revival in anticipation of the 'second coming'. Followers of religious groups around the world prepared for the 'return'. German Templars settled at the base of Mt. Carmel in Israel in anticipation of the imminent arrival of their Lord. In the United States William Miller, a student of the bible, predicted the return of Christ for 1844. His followers were called Millerites. Later, when the Millerites lost hope in Christ's return, some of them morphed into the Adventists.

Followers of Islam predicted the emergence of the Twelfth Imam in the year 1260 A.H. of the Muslim calendar. This corresponds to the year 1844 A.D. in the Christian calendar.

Members of the Baha'i Faith believe that Christ did return, in the spirit, in the form of a dual manifestation from God, beginning with "The Bab", meaning "the gate" in 1844 as predicted, and subsequently with "Baha'u'llah" or the "Glory of God", who declared his mission in 1863.

All of this anticipation created a worldwide religious fervor. In the United States many Christians conducted revival meetings across the country.

But Christianity at the time was heavily divided into many sects. There were many so-called preachers who used this fervor to milk the believers who were eager for enlightenment and guidance. Joseph Smith was fed up with the divergent religious claims of the religious pundits of his time. As a religious man he apparently sought the truth about spiritual reality. He read scripture a great deal and prayed for guidance. Whether inspired by God or in a self-induced state of meditation, Smith might have believed he was led to the gold tablets by an angel. For all we know, maybe he was. But most likely he was exploring the woods and stumbled across their hiding place. As a boy, I used to go for long walks in the woods myself. It's a very spiritual experience.

Smith could have persuaded a local native to try to translate the pictographs in the Walum Olum. The native probably wasn't familiar with all of the drawings. Some of those Nyana studied are similar to the universal sign language used by the various North American native tribes to communicate, prior to the large-scale infiltration of the Europeans. Others look like altered Greek letters or Egyptian Hieroglyphs."

"Yeah. But there's something strange about the pictographs in my working copy from the Panther Chamber." said Nyana. "I need to continue my historical research of the period for more clues."

"How's that?" asked Kirk.

"Well, sequential characters seem to jump from one to the other, skipping vital information. It's like writing a cogent sentence then randomly removing words here and there in the linear text. It's fragmented, like trying to read shorthand. I don't know. I'll keep working on it."

"You'll figure it out hon." But in this case the so-called translator could have made up what he didn't know, just to appease Smith." continued Randall. "If you're doing contract work, you always give the customer what he wants. Considering the religious fervor at the time, and that the translator might have been a Christianized native, he might have filled in the blanks with the Bible stories he learned in church. Thus, Smith thought he had found a new version of the Bible and went on from there to preach it.

One legend has it that Smith was told by the angel not to form yet another religion because the religious renewal would be left up to Christ when He returned. Well, Smith had many followers and his 'church' went by various names. But he didn't exactly start another formalized religion. Unfortunately, his successor, Brigham Young, did."

"The Church of Jesus Christ of Latter-day Saints; the Mormons." said Lucy.

Chapter 7
Plan "A"

"Based on our research to date," said Randall, "Nyana and I believe the Lenape tablets probably are not solid gold, but might be an alloy of gold and copper called 'Tumbaga' in Mesoamerica. It was used throughout the Americas and elsewhere. Gold itself is too soft for archival purposes."

"You said are?" asked Kirk. "You're talking now as if they actually exist?"

"That's our working hypothesis." replied Randall. "You guys interested in checking it out?"

"Whattya think Lucy?" asked Kirk.

"Well, the trip has been fun so far; beautiful scenery here. What else have we got going?"

"Were in. What's our next step?"

"Let me give you some more background first." said Randall. "Most archaeologists speculate that the mound builders were members of the Adena, Hopewell and Fort Ancient cultures dating from around 800 B.C. to 1200 A.D. But our research, based upon information from the Panther Chamber, suggests that the mound builders were more ancient than the Lenape, possibly a race called the Allegewi. They built the mounds over sacred areas and may have used them for multiple purposes, in addition to their spiritual significance. They may have also served as say, survey markers used to navigate from one place to another. That's just wild speculation, but it's unlikely that any culture would go to all that trouble to construct massive structures just for one reason. There are thousands of mounds in the Ohio area alone. Somehow they knew that a meteorite struck at Serpent Mound. They may have been able to monitor magnetic anomalies. You can do that today with simple instruments, such as a metal needle tied to a thin string or length of hair. Remember, the ancients weren't as ignorant as we think. But if our working hypothesis about the Panther Chamber is correct, then the Allegewi may have been guided to the Serpent by a prophet or Manifestation from God, or given that knowledge of these locations by some other means. The sacred places we've cataloged in other areas thus far have all been marked by a meterorite or asteroid hit. The Allegewi were later driven out, apparently escaping down the Mississippi Valley and into historic oblivion.

We need to proceed systematically. You and Lucy need to focus on Serpent Mound. Get all the information about it that you can. Let's see if we can find the gold tablets. We've got some equipment on the way. Good Luck."

Lucy excused herself to use the ladies room while Kirk photographed Serpent Mound and the surrounding area from ground level.

"We need to see if there are any artifacts left in or around the Serpent." said Kirk as he and Lucy later strolled toward the parking lot.

"Well that should be easy enough." said Lucy. "All we have to do is bring in a backhoe and start digging."

"We could do that, but I think we may encounter some resistance from the park service. How about if we us a less invasive method?"

"Well my dad's ground penetrating radar worked well in Saudi Arabia, but it's very expensive and bulky. As I recall it took dad a long time to setup to get accurate results. And he had to take the data back to analyze it with the university computer. He had to wait to time-share. He was able to speed up the process when he connected with Randall, who had access to a Cray supercomputer at that time. But it still took a long time."

"That's true. But he was using first generation electronics. There now exists a new generation of GPR. The whole system fits in a moderately sized Pelican case, uses batteries or fuel cells for portable operation without a generator, and has remote wireless sensors to record data over a wide area. We can interface it with the mainframe at the British Museum to generate real time data interpretation. Randall was salivating over the specs when he read them to me at our headquarters at the Museum. We were previewing a lot of new equipment that nobody else has yet. We can use the GPR to quickly analyze the Serpent Mount without offending too many people."

"Great. I don't suppose we can pick up one at the local radio shack?"

"Not quite, but close. We'll drive up about three hours north of here. It's a good thing we got started early. There's a great restaurant on the way where we can get the best apple pie in the country."

"What does apple pie have to do with Ground Penetrating Radar? Or are you just hungry again?"

"I'm always hungry for good home-cooked food. But the restaurant is just outside of Kidron, in Amish Country. There's a store in Kidron called Lehman's. They're reputed to carry everything. They supply a lot of materials to the local Amish."

"The Amish use a lot of GPR units? What are they looking for, horseshoes?"

"I don't think so. But we should be able to pick up one of the new GPR units there, and get some great apple pie. You do like apple pie don't you?"

"A la mode, please."

As Kirk and Lucy drove north to Kidron, Ohio.

"I've just accessed lehmans.com on the net." said Lucy. "They sell wood burning stoves, hand-crank apple peelers, milk cans and gas powered refrigerators, among other off-the-grid stuff. Tell me again how we're going to pickup a state of the art GPR system from an Amish supply store?"

"You'll see. But first, apple pie. I'm hungry, aren't you?" Kirk said as they pulled into the Amish Crescent restaurant parking lot.

"Interesting name. I assume they serve homemade crescent rolls?"

"Probably. But the name comes from the fact that the owner is an expatriate Muslim cleric who was run out of Iran for preaching tolerance toward other religions, specifically the Baha'is, who are severely persecuted there. His interpretation of the Koran is that it requires tolerance toward other religions. Indeed, Mohammed protected other religions. That's part of the Hadith, or Muslim tradition. That view is not shared by the more powerful Islamic fascists there. They kind of made up their own religion. So he high-tailed it out of there before he ended up in that hellhole where I was held."

"So Muslim clerics make a good apple pie?"

"I'm guessing not. But don't worry. All the cooks are Amish."

"Where do they get the apples in the spring?" asked Lucy.

"They're from down under."

"Oh, Australia."

"No. From down under the restaurant. They have a large root cellar in which they store locally grown apples for the winter in a controlled atmosphere. We're lucky because we'll have some of the last ones available until September. They're still in excellent condition. They make pies with rhubarb, then strawberries, then cherries and peaches, then apples; whatever is in season or can be stored properly. The menu changes with the harvest to reflect locally grown, in season or stored foods. They import only spices."

"How do you know all this stuff?"

"These are my old haunts. Remember, I was born and raised here in Ohio."

"I suppose this is one of the places where you brought your old girlfriends?"

"No. This is where I brought my young girlfriends. You're the only old girlfriend I've had."

"You're living on borrowed time mister."

The restaurant was a low, steeply sloped metal-roofed rectangular building with a soffit that extended over the grey concrete sidewalk that hugged the foundation. This served to protect customers from the heavy rains generated by the strong thunderstorms that frequently visited the area. The pastel green stained cedar shingled facade was reminiscent of the siding on the Embassy where Kirk and Randall lived off campus while attending Kent State University. Low-slung bright-green shiny leafed boxwood, hedged the sidewalk on the parking lot side, while bright, blood-orange miniature marigolds stood at attention along its outer perimeter.

Lucy hesitated as she reluctantly walked under the Crescent shaped sign, remembering her sojourn in Saudi Arabia.

Inside, they were met by a young woman wearing traditional Amish garb of a pleated long black skirt and white blouse with a small close-fitting white hat and a spotless white apron adorned with stylized pansies. She escorted them to a small booth located along an outside wall. As they approached, the dark red Naugahyde upholstery and the red and white gingham fabric tablecloth appeared vibrant in the sunlight.

The tall, old, white cased windows were framed with sun bleached beige colored lace curtains.

After a filling dinner of fried chicken, locally grown vegetables and mashed potatoes, Lucy and Kirk savored the best apple pie they ever ate.

"I'm stuffed." said Kirk. "Let's waddle over to the bed and breakfast nearby and spend the night. We'll go to the store tomorrow and see about our GPR unit."

Chapter 8
Flashbacks

The nearby Bed & Breakfast consisted of a series of eight small log cabins, forming a 'U' shaped courtyard facing a small paved parking lot. The grounds were spotlessly clean. Tall, late spring perennial tulips stood at attention in alternating rows of red, white and quasi blue along a paved walk. Just before the first cabin, and off to the left, stood a small office with a sloping shed type roof. The entrance faced the road and invited its guests in with a traditional 'welcome' mat. Kirk and Lucy checked in.

"We'd like a cabin for the night." said Kirk to the old woman sitting behind the desk.

Her granny glasses were sitting on the end of her nose and about to dive into the newspaper she was reading. "With or without water?" she asked without looking up.

"Huh?" said Kirk in surprise.

"Just kidding." She said as she raised both her face and voice. "They all have bathrooms. But I suggest you take a shower early…or late if you want hot water. After you move in we'll be full for the night. Good thing you got here when you did. A lot of tourists showing up for the Apple Blossom Festival this weekend."

Crabapple trees crowned with red blossoms stood guard alongside the pergola entrance to the winding path which led to the cabins. This path reminded Lucy of the Serpent Mound. As they walked together Kirk noticed a tall lilac bush leaning against their cabin. He remembered the Jacaranda tree in the courtyard where he was imprisoned in Teheran; where Susan's body was dropped at his feet. Kirk tried to shake the thought from his mind, moving his head side to side rapidly like a swimmer trying to clear his ears of water.

"Are you alright sweetie?" asked Lucy.

"Yeah! Yeah. I'm okay. Just trying to get away from a bee."

"Oh. I didn't see her. There must be a lot of them around with all these blossoms."

"Yeah… blossoms… Here's our room."

The cabin was relatively small, simple and clean. The pine furniture was sturdy and well made by local Amish craftsmen, as if it was designed to last for a lifetime. The queen sized bed faced the door and window and divided the room. The headboard was a thick, hand-carved frame over which a large inexpensive painting stood guard. The pastoral scene contained the obligatory cows and chickens, a recurring theme in local design. A tall dresser with six drawers stood off to the left. Window curtains were plain patterned white lace, hanging onto a straight brass rod secured above the latticed window. A small pull down shade provided privacy. The entrance to the small bathroom was off to the right of the bed. Nightstands, topped with a small brass lamp with a white fabric shade, rested by each side of the bed. The warm spring breeze entered the open window and freshened the room. This cabin reminded Kirk of the room in which he first slept after Harry rescued him. But painful memories were rapidly surfacing.

Little was said that evening. Kirk seemed withdrawn; a bit more contemplative than usual, so Lucy didn't force the conversation. He and Lucy hit the sack early. They had a long day today and an even longer one planned for tomorrow.

Kirk's mind was running at full bore. Images rolled in and out of his consciousness as if he was flipping the pages of an illustrated novel; his life story. He had a hard time getting to sleep. He got up and sat on the hardwood floor. After he applied the meditation techniques that Harry's personal trainer taught him, he was finally able to control his thoughts and quiet his mind enough to climb back into bed and nod off. Slowly the scene unfolded:

There was a lone tree where I was standing. A jacaranda... No! A
maple, oak, elm... just leafing out... young woman looking at the
ground...Susan, no... someone else... a stranger looking for keys...
trying to get away...the national guard started to move...someone
gave the order to...march up the hill...

"Kirk! Kirk! Wake up! Are you alright. You scared me. You were yelling."

"I guess I had a bad dream. I'm sorry I woke you."

"That's okay. It's time to get up anyway. We should talk about it later huh?"

"Yeah."

Chapter 9
The Amish Connection

After a hearty breakfast at the Amish Crescent, the couple pulled into the parking lot of Lehman's store. Lucy had a look of confusion on her face as they walked inside. The store looked like a large antique red barn loaded with products that Lucy thought hadn't been made any longer.

"Wow! We just walked into the nineteenth century. Oh look Kirk. A manure spreader. You and Randall should go in together and buy one. You both could use it. On second thought, that's only a small walk-behind unit. You'll need the big one we passed outside."

"Yeah, and here's something for you, the 'Ball Blue Book of Preserving Food'. So you can learn to 'can' it." replied Kirk sarcastically. "But don't let it fool you. Every product in this store is in use today. None of the cheap plastic Chinese crap either. They sell high quality materials that appeal to back-to-the-land folks all over the world as well as the local Amish and Mennonites."

Kirk finally approached the main counter and asked for the operations manager. A tall, thin, muscular, middle-aged man with a long gray beard, a blue and green plaid shirt, suspenders with blue jeans and a black baseball hat that said 'Toys R Us', walked slowly out of the small office behind the counter area.

"How may I help you sir?" he asked in a sincere, friendly manner.

"I'm in the market for a Tesla 5000, Portable Ground Penetrating Radar Unit."

"You're in luck sir. We have one unit left in stock." The manager said with a straight face. "Would you like the fuel cell power system with that?"

"Yes, please." Kirk replied as Lucy took in the proceedings with a look of incredulity on her face.

The manager set off to the back room and returned shortly.

"Here you go sir. That'll be ten million dollars please. That includes taxes and shipping charges."

"Do you give senior citizen discounts?"

"Are you sixty-five sir?"

"Not for a few years yet."

"I'm sorry sir. We do give a five percent discount, but you have to be sixty five."

"No problem. I have an expense account. Do you take credit cards?"

"VISA or Mastercard sir."

"VISA. With this purchase I ought to get enough frequent flyer miles to go to the moon." Kirk said as he ran his card through the scanner.

"Sign here please. Oh, and sir, with every ten million dollar purchase we're giving away this wind up LED flashlight."

"Thanks."

Do you need help getting loaded sir?"

"He can do that on his own." Lucy cut in sarcastically.

"I think we can get it, thanks." Kirk said as he handed Lucy the fuel cell power unit and picked up the Black Pelican case with the GPR unit.

Lucy followed him back to the car. Kirk burst out laughing as he saw the look on Lucy's face.

"O.K. smartass." Lucy said. "What just happened?"

"I'm sorry babe. I couldn't help but play it straight as long as Jerry in there went along with it. You should have seen the look on your face. Randall called me back when you were in the bathroom at the visitor's center at Serpent Mound. He told me that Amid arranged for the Radar unit to be shipped to us and gave me the specifics. They shipped it to Lehman's, because Amid's Uncle's company has been doing business with Lehman's for years, purchasing hand-made Amish quilts that are traded to the Arabs for hand-made Arab rugs. Jerry back there is an old friend of Amid. The GPR unit was paid for by Harry Stratford when he purchased it in Egypt. The Egyptians developed it with a grant from the Stratford Foundation, so they could use them to analyze the pyramids and other structures. Also, I don't really have a ten million dollar limit on my VISA. Randall said that Jerry has a good sense of humor and would go along with any nonsense I started."

"At my expense. Thank you very much."

"I'm glad you have a good sense of humor."

"After our harrowing experiences in Arabia and the Sudan, I mellowed out a bit. And besides, you have an intoxicating influence on me."

"You mean like a fine wine?"

"Well, maybe like a glass of hard cider." Lucy said as they kissed.

"Time to head back to the Serpent, or Randall and Nayana will have a hissy fit. If anything's there, we ought to see it with this new radar. We can plan our sets today then get started with the readings in the morning. That will take the rest of the day. There's a bed and breakfast nearby the mound where we can spend the night discussing lip locking procedures in detail."

"I like that plan."

"Did you coordinate our work with Nyana?" asked Kirk.

"Yes. As an official representative of the Indian Institute of the Arts, Nyana contacted the Ohio Historical Society which operates the museum. They gave her permission to allow us to run the GPR for one day, as long as we didn't dig anywhere."

"Too bad Nyana isn't driving today. We could be back at the Serpent in an hour." said Kirk as he laughed out loud.

"Yeah but our hair would be standing straight up. She's a maniac when she gets behind the wheel. Randall almost freaked out when she drove under that elephant outside of New Delhi."

Lucy and Kirk drove back to Serpent Mound State Park and scoped out the locations for the sensors and receiver of the GPR. They made contact with the Ranger on duty there, as well as the Ohio Historical Society supervisor, Sherry Thomas, so they would be able to start shooting early the next day.

"I don't think there's anything of interest there." said Sherry. "But we welcome any data that might add to our knowledge base. After all, nobody really knows the extent of Mr. Putnam's excavation. He did such a thorough job of restoring the site afterwards."

"We'll make sure you get a copy of our analysis, Sherry." said Lucy.

"Good luck with your work. I'll be around tomorrow if you need anything." Sherry said as she walked back to her office.

"This thing is long Kirk. We'll have to run a number of shots to explore the whole Serpent. Plus, we'll have to shoot the two burial mounds separately."

"Agreed. I'm glad you had the experience of helping your dad shoot in Arabia. Randall forced me to study the manual for this unit while we were back at the British Museum, but I've never used it before. In fact, nobody has because it's so new."

"My dad's equipment was primitive compared to this, but the theory is the same. Send electromagnetic waves through the ground and monitor the reflections."

"Very much like the seismic imaging used in the oilfield to find structures that may act as reservoirs for petroleum, but using radar pulses instead of acoustic. The early units like those used by your dad wouldn't work very well here because they wouldn't penetrate very far in clay soils. But this unit is much more powerful and the receiver more sensitive. Interfacing it with Randall's computers will produce a detailed three dimensional image like a CAT scanner used to image humans in three dimensions.

I'm not sure what we'll find. Apparently Frederick Ward Putnam spent three years excavating this site starting in 1886. But Randall and Nyana want to be absolutely sure the tablets aren't here, before we go off on another tangent."

"O.K. we've got our plan together. It's getting dark soon so we should head to the Bed & Breakfast for the night."

The Bed and Breakfast was an old blue-gray shingled three story Victorian House with white trim. The entrance was across a large porch encompassing the front and flanked by tall Arborvitae evergreens. In front of the porch, extending to ground level, a dark green latticework backed a flowerbed filled with vibrant, multicolored pansies whose oversized faces surveyed the new arrivals. An antique hardwood and leaded glass door welcomed the visitors and invited them in. Inside, Kirk took a seat on an oversized stuffed chair in a secluded front corner while Lucy checked them in. He decided to make a phone call he had been putting off.

"This is Kirk, 'call Harry'." Kirk said to the phone.

The phone seemed to blink interminably, until at last.

"Kirk, nice to hear from you."

"Glad you were available Harry"

"Calls from the team members are high priority Kirk, especially yours. Sorry it took so long to answer. Have you called that shrink yet?"

"Not yet, I'm doing O.K. Being with Lucy makes things easier. She understands."

"Still having those flashbacks?"

"Not as much. You got my update? When we're working on a project I feel alright. I think we're doing something important. When I'm with the team; that seems to stop the flashes."

"Don't wait too long. I don't want you getting squirrelly on me. When I pulled you out of that prison you were nearly in a vegetative state. You don't want to unload on Lucy. That's what professionals are for."

"I'll make the call if I get too out of whack."

"Kirk. The idea is to make the call before you get out of whack. I gave you the code. That will put you right through to Helen."

"Thanks for caring, Harry. Here comes Lucy."

"Put her on."

Kirk handed the phone to Lucy and took the opportunity to look at the rack of postcards nearby.

"Hey Lucy. Harry here. How are you sweetheart?"

"Great. It's warm and sunny and all the trees are coming into bloom. But Kirk is trying to fatten me up with all the eating we've been doing. If I eat another piece of cheese I'm going to blow up. How about you Harry?"

"Fine dear. It's great to hear your voice. You sound happy."

"I am, more than I could imagine."

"Any problems?"

"No. we're set for tomorrow at Serpent Mound. I think that…"

"No Lucy! I'm talking about Kirk."

"I ah…I'm not sure."

"I set up a call he needs to make. A woman I've known all my life. She can help him, even just speaking with him on the phone. She's good at getting to the root of the problem."

"I'll talk to him. I promise."

Chapter 10
Team-Recovery

The next day Lucy and Kirk set up the equipment early and spent most of the day running shots with the GPR. They used their satellite phone to transmit the data to the mainframe computer at their British Museum headquarters.

"Randall, did you receive the transmission?"

"Clear and complete Kirk. Good job. We already started to process the data. I should know if anything is down there in a matter of hours. By the way, Harry Stratford and company has given us a designation, probably for tax purposes. As of now our little group will be known as 'The Recovery Team'."

"Doesn't sound too sexy." replied Kirk.

"Well it sounds better than the 'geriatric ancient relic chasers club'. And it makes sense since we're trying to recover the artifacts that match the placeholders in the Panther Chamber."

"Touche."

"I hear the Maple and Oak trees are in their full glory, and the Buckeye trees will soon be in full bloom. I remember the beautiful multi-colored blossoms the Buckeyes produce. I haven't seen those for years." said Randall.

"Well come on over. The only thing better than the apple pie here is the weather."

"We might have to, depending on the results of those radar shots. I'll call you back later. Relax and enjoy the sunshine."

Chapter 11
Connections

After a late dinner Lucy and Kirk were sitting in the porch swing at the bed and breakfast, enjoying the sunset. After a period of silence, Lucy put her arm around Kirk and said.

"Sweetie; I've had a few bad dreams about the Janjaweed helicopter we destroyed in the Sudan. I was shocked by the damage we did to those soldiers with our shrapnel pistols. The gunner and the pilot were just young men. I keep trying to justify it because I know they would have killed us a second later if we hadn't fired at them. But it's still so hard to take a human life."

"But they killed Jonathan; not only did they take your husband from you, but they ended the life of a doctor who helped the refugees survive until they could return to their homes. And they were on their way to do more of the same. They might have killed your friend Linda at the IDP camp."

"I know. But I'm still very uncomfortable with the thought. It wears on me from time to time."

"If it didn't, you wouldn't be human."

"Having you by my side makes it easier. I hope I have the same effect on you."

"Oh you do."

"Then tell me about that nightmare you had the other night. When you woke up you were visibly shaken."

"Ahh... I don't know. I just seemed to have all these images running through my mind. I tried to focus on other things, more pleasant thoughts... you and me and our current quest. But I had a terrible time trying to get to sleep. Something triggered a bad dream."

"Harry said he knew of someone you might call."

"Well you know Harry, hovering over us like an old dog."

"Taking both his hands in hers, and looking intently into Kirk's eyes, Lucy whispered strongly....I love you."

After a few moments of silence Kirk responded.

"I'll make the call."

Chapter 12
Analysis

"Phone." said Kirk addressing the black satellite phone. "Call Dr. Helen Smith in Chicago, Illinois."

A moment later a computerized voice answered. "Dr. Smith's office. For office hours push 1; To leave a message push 2, for emergencies only, push 3 and then the pound key, then leave a message and a contact number. Clients with codes please press the asterisk and speak the code."

No asterisk or other keys on this thing. Let me try something else. Kirk thought.

"Asterisk." said Kirk. "Stratford team #1."

After about a minute a human voice came on.

"Please standby for Dr. Smith, Mr. Michaels."

A few long minutes passed until.

"Doctor Helen Smith. Are you still there Mister Michaels?"

"Yeah, yes."

"Harry said you wanted to speak with me. Of course he gave me no details except to say you were in the field working on a very important project. I prefer to see people in person, but I specialize in remote clients. Some of my professional associates criticize me for my approach. I tell them that if a surgeon can now perform an operation from thousands of miles away, I can shrink heads by remote also. Do you have the time to talk now?"

"Only if you promise not to shrink my head too much."

"I'll try." she laughed. "Okay. Talk to me."

Kirk gave Dr. Smith a brief biography and background information, describing his nightmares in detail. He refrained from relating his activities concerning the Panther Chamber and events since, except to say that he has a job that occasionally entails highly stressful activities.

"Kirk. I sense that you're not telling me everything. That's okay for now, but if you are unable to resolve your conflicts fairly soon, you'll have to come clean. Based upon what you've told me, I think the layout of that bed and breakfast near Kidron brought back enough images of Teheran to trigger some flashbacks. We need to focus on the true nature of the trigger though. Each flashback is slightly different. That indicates to me that your mind is trying to heal itself; to reset reality."

"So I'm not living in a real world?"

"Yes." Dr. Smith laughed. "Such as it is. But your dreams are trying to help you refocus on the event that you suppressed. I hate to say take two aspirin and call me in the morning. But that's all I can do for you now. You may have to suffer a few more flashbacks. If you do, or if there are any other changes, call me."

Chapter 13
Momentum

The next day Randall called with the results of the GPR analysis.

"Kirk , bad news. It looks like Putnam pretty much cleaned house. I'm quite sure Kirk. There's nothing of our interest at Serpent Mound. James MacDonald and I ran those GPR images through my special enhancement algorithm, the same one I used to locate the Panther Chamber. We got a clear view of everything down to the level of the crypto-explosive bedrock. There's nothing there except a few broken residual arrowheads. If the artifact exists, it's elsewhere."

"Thank you for keeping my father involved Randall. After spending so much time in prison and faced with the death of my mother, he needs something to focus on." said Lucy.

"I couldn't keep him away." said Randall. "Besides, he can keep track of you while he works with us. His years of experience makes him a valuable member of the team."

"What's next?" asked Kirk.

"Based on the information we have, or rather don't have, the only logical conclusion at this point is that either the tablets don't exist, or the Lenape never recovered them from Smith." said Randall

"If Smith still had them, then he took them on his journey to Salt Lake City, yes?" asked Kirk.

"No." responded Nyana. "Based on our conversations, I researched Joseph Smith and the Mormon migration. He and his followers moved to Ohio, Missouri, and, in the spring of 1839 to Nauvoo, Illinois. Smith was jailed in Carthage, Illinois. He was killed on June 27, 1844, along with his brother.

But the Mormons under Brigham Young continued on to Salt Lake. Someone else could have taken the tablets there.

"Possibly." responded Randall skeptically. "But they had a long and erratic journey to Utah. The tablets could have been lost along the way. Or the people who jailed, and subsequently killed, Joseph Smith could have stolen them. That would expand our search parameters significantly. Some dork could even have melted them down and sold them as simple gold."

"Not likely." said Nyana. "The alloy wouldn't have assayed as pure gold. And even a person of questionable intelligence would have recognized the artifact as something of value."

"But if the Mormons had them now, why wouldn't they show them to the world? Any ideas, anyone?" asked Kirk.

"Don't know." Any ideas ladies?" Randall asked of Lucy and Nyana.

"Well." said Nyana. "I translated a bit of the place-keeping copy of the tablets, that we found in the Holographic chamber. But my work is full of holes. I can only fill them by looking at the original. But so far it looks like a biblically modeled representation of the creation myth, Genesis, that predates Christianity by millennia. It also hints of some sort of long journey or migration. Maybe the Mormons don't want to show it to the world because it doesn't prove their religion as a renewal of Christianity as they say it is."

"There's another possibility." suggested Lucy. "Even if they have them, maybe they don't have an accurate translation. They don't know what it says."

"That's good Lucy." said Nyana. "I don't want to, how do you say it, blow my own horn? But considering the difficulty I've had translating what little I have so far, even with the aid of my translation algorithm, I believe it would be, at best, very difficult for anyone else to translate it. And if someone had approached any of my colleagues anywhere on the planet, I would have heard about it. The Mormons may be keeping it under wraps until they can be sure of getting an accurate translation."

"That makes sense." said Kirk. "Nobody could anticipate the final results of an accurate, scholarly interpretation."

"I was aided by some of the pictograms on the 'Lenape Stone'. I plugged them into my algorithm along with other pictograms found among the Lenape."

"What's the 'Lenape Stone'." asked Kirk.

"It's a kind of breastplate found in two pieces in a field in 1872 and 1881 respectively, in Bucks County, Pennsylvania, by a local farmer. It depicts a battle between natives and a woolly mammoth.

The individuals who found the pieces cleaned them a number of times, so anthropologists were unable to run an accurate scientific analysis to determine authenticity. But the inscriptions look authentic, and more importantly, correspond with Lenape legend. So even if the stone itself is phony, the faker may have copied the pictograms from other, original materials. In either case, I may later be able to use my software application to determine the authenticity of the Lenape Stone and other native American artifacts. This type of pictogram rendition was often used as a mnemonic in various tribal celebrations to aid one's memory when they were singing, say, legends or histories. The same relationship may exist between linguistics and pictograms with the Gold tablets. We know from modern brain research that a story can be encoded in our long term memories by song.

"This program of yours sounds impressive." said Lucy.

"It should be. I spent many years designing and refining it along with a lot of help from various colleagues." replied Nayana. Unfortunately, I haven't adapted it to turn the pictograms into sound yet. That would require an unbelievable amount of work. I'll let that for someone else. My goal here is to fashion a reasonably accurate narrative from the pictograms alone. Lenape historians can fill in the oral history later.

"Do you have a name for your program." asked Lucy.

"Yes. I call it Rose."

"Oh that's cute." said Lucy. "A short form for the Rosetta stone which had three languages carved on it, Classical Greek, Demotic and Hieroglyphic. That was the key that enabled researchers to translate Egyptian Hieroglyphics accurately for the first time. That's very appropriate Nya."

"Well no. Actually, I named it after my Aunt Rose who helped to subsidize my college education. But I was inspired by the Rosetta stone. I have spent much time just staring at it lately in the British Museum. It served as my muse for the current project."

"O.K. If they exist, How can we determine the location of the Tablets?" asked Kirk, bringing the discussion back to the main subject.

"Unless we want to chase a bunch of dead ends, we have to narrow our chase to the most probable case, that is, that the Mormons have them, or know where they are." said Nyana. "If that assumption is wrong then we go back to square one. So I think we should proceed as if that is correct. I thought we might find information as to the whereabouts of the artifact by accessing the archives in the Mormon Family History Library at Salt Lake City, Utah."

"Did you log onto the archives and check it out?" asked Lucy.

"I did, but no luck. It's not in the digitized information that's open to the public. I contacted the librarian at the Mormon headquarters there. I asked her point blank if I could get information on the legend of the 'Gold Tablets'. She said only Mormon elders can access the vault that holds the closed stacks containing that information."

"Where are the closed stacks located, exactly?" asked Kirk.

"They're in the Granite Mountain Records Vault in the Wasatch Mountains southeast of Salt Lake City." said Nyana. "The index should be in there too, so we can use it to more easily access any records referring to the artifact."

"Well, if the Mormons won't allow access, we'll have to break into the Vault and go through the closed stacks. We need to look there." said Randall.

"Don't be so eager to commit another felony my friend." said Kirk. You almost died the last time."

"That was close. But I don't think the Mormons will chase us down with rocket fire from black helicopters like the Janjaweed did in Darfur." said Randall. If they catch us they'll just talk us to death. So if everyone is in agreement, let's go to Salt Lake City…. Hearing no objections, the motion to stick our necks out again passes unanimously. Now what do we know about the Mormon Archives there?"

"Not much. But we have a contact in Salt Lake." said Nyana. "We'll meet you guys there. This is definitely going to require a team effort."

Chapter 14
Intrigue

The tall, forty-something, muscular man, wearing an expensive gray suit, and carrying an aggressive demeanor along with a 9mm, threw open the thick wooden sliding doors.

"Come in Mr. Sanders. And close the doors."

He marched carefully into a large drawing room that strongly resembled an antique museum. Shelves laden with carvings, figurines and assorted paraphernalia covered two walls. The other walls held leather-bound books and tightly wound scrolls that one might expect to have seen on loan from the Library at Alexandria. Several small, brown, round wooden tables displayed engraved stone tablets. Large Persian rugs obscured the dark hardwood floor. A short, black, tower type computer with three adjacent thirty inch wide panoramic displays, rested on an excessively large, dark colored African walnut desk. The displays illuminated the otherwise dark room with an eerie glow, casting shadows onto grey walls. In the corner, with his back to the door, stood a robust, elderly presence that filled the room along with the smoke of his Cuban Cohiba cigar. He slowly turned and said nothing.

"Yes sir?"

"My RSS feeds picked up an article written by a local paper in Southern Ohio. Someone is nosing around Serpent Mound. It seems they ran a Ground Penetrating Radar analysis. See what you can find out. I don't like it... don't like it at all. Here's the background information."

"I'll take care of it Mr. Penn." He said as he picked up the manila folder.

He backed away, slowly turned and quickly exited to the main corridor. Then he accessed a small, sparsely furnished security office off to the left of the foyer. After spending some time reading the information he pulled out his cell phone. He manually punched in a familiar number, since he was careful to keep nothing in the phone's memory.

Shortly a voice answered."Nice to hear from you. It's been a long time."

"You guys available?"

"Depends."

"Here's the job. Someone's looking for something at the Serpent."

"Treasure hunting kids again?"

"Ground Penetrating Radar, not metal detectors."

"Really? Who?"

"Two PhD's. One is a nosy photographer. He gave a lecture at Kent State University recently. He spent some time in a prison in Iran.

"Why?"

"For being a nosy photographer. The other one is some broad who used to work for the Clinton Administration. Very competent/brainy; easy on the eyes. The republicans ran her off when they staged their coup d' etat in 2000. They didn't want any advisors around who could think."

"But they used Ground Penetrating Radar. That's pretty serious snooping. Nothing's there right?"

"Right. We cleaned house years ago. We never found anything."

"What about that Putnam stuff in Boston?"

"All clear, just a bunch of arrowheads, spear points, pipes and a clay marker. We never found anything that would allow the indians to claim any lands. If we had, we would have destroyed it right away; on standing orders."

"From old man Penn? That son-of-a bitch will do anything to protect his legacy."

"And his money. His bank account would be the first to go if the natives pushed through a new settlement act to compensate for the lands his ancestors stole under the 'Walking Purchase' fraud."

"Yeah, and the government would have to pony up a couple billion too."

"More like a couple of trillion now, with the price of land plus interest for almost three hundred years. Remember the briefing I gave you guys. The Lenape owned parts of New Jersey, New York City Pennsylvania...."

"Yeah we get it."

"You better check these guys out a little closer."

"We'll take it. Time and expenses?"

"Done. But don't be padding your account. No more five star hotels, understand?"

"Yeah. Like there are a bunch of five star accommodations in Hooterville country."

"Keep in contact."

Chapter 15
The Walking Purchase

"The 'Walking Purchase' fraud, Kirk?" asked Lucy.

"That's how this whole thing got started. The Lenape originally agreed to share their lands with the new settlers. William Penn legitimately purchased some land from the Indians and was highly respected for the way he treated them. But in 1737, his sons Thomas and John produced an old deed, purportedly signed in 1686 by three Delaware Indian chiefs, selling land extending from the northern boundary of the 'Neshaminy Purchase' as far as a man can walk in a day and a half and then eastward to the Delaware River. The signatories to the deed were all long dead and the deed was considered to be an altered copy of an old agreement allowing the temporary use of land, not the sale. But the natives reluctantly agreed to honor the deed. They thought the walkers would follow an Indian path along the Delaware River, stopping to rest and eat periodically.

But the instigators cleared a straight path and hired professional walkers who started out from what is now Wrightstown, Pennsylvania. The walkers covered a much greater distance than a regular man would, effectively cheating the natives out of a huge amount of land, about 1200 square miles. The Delaware refused to vacate the area when they realized they had been cheated, again. But they were ultimately removed, unfortunately, with the help of the Iroquois Indians who had long oppressed the Delaware. The Lenape moved west into Central Pennsylvania, then into the Ohio territory and into Michigan, Indiana, Arkansas, Kansas, Oklahoma and other areas as they were forced out of their lands over time by white settlers."

Chapter 16
Arrival

L ucy and Kirk flew to Salt Lake and arrived that evening. On the way, Kirk called Harry to update him. Upon arrival, they were surprised to find a limousine waiting for them at the airport. The driver took them to the Grand America Hotel.

When they checked in, they found they were pre-registered for an entire luxury suite. The porter escorted them to their suite and made sure everything was satisfactory. When Kirk tried to tip him, the porter declined and said that everything had been taken care of. Kirk and Lucy wondered what was going on as they heard a knock at the door. When the opened it, Amid al Rahid entered.

"How do you like it?" he asked as he waved his hands around.

"I take it this lap of luxury into which we have fallen is financed from the bank vaults of Harry Stratford." asked Kirk.

"Yes, Harry has too much money and I feel obligated to relieve him of his burden.." said Amid.

"…so he will become a more spiritual person." Everyone said in unison.

"Amid, welcome to Salt Lake City." Lucy said as they hugged.

"Wouldn't have missed it for the free world."

"How did you get into the country?" asked Kirk. "I thought you were on the no fly list?"

"Oh that. It was a simple misunderstanding. The Chinese were shipping some electronic components used in the guidance systems of surface-to-air antiaircraft missiles to the Sudanese army at Khartoum. They had to pass through the Port of Sudan where my uncle's company arranged to off load them and prepare them for continuing on to Khartoum. Since I work there, the U.S. government became upset and put us all on the list."

"I wonder why?"

"But there was no real problem. You see, my uncle's technicians added GPS tracking chips to the components, so the CIA could pinpoint antiaircraft strongholds used by the Sudanese Army. But the CIA refused to release that information to Homeland Security so I could get off the no fly list. The CIA doesn't like Homeland security. But it worked out alright. Now I'm not only off the list, but I'm a preferred risk so I can zip right through security."

"How did you perform that miracle?" asked Lucy. "It took Senator Al Gore a week to get off the list? They love to add names, but never to remove them."

"Well, it turns out that after the 9-11 attacks, Homeland Security was assembled so quickly that they outsourced much of their work; radiation detectors to China, pre-employment background checks to Israeli security..."

"What's wrong with that? It seems efficient. Israeli security has the most efficient background check business. And China currently produces the best radiation detectors on the market."

"...and upgrade, expansion and maintenance of the no fly database system to a security firm in England, which outsourced it to Bangalore, India, which outsourced it to ...Saudi Arabia, specifically the bin Laden group." continued Amid.

"Now you're putting us on Amid?" said Lucy.

"I wish I was, but no. And it gets better. Outsourcing the no fly database from Bangalore to the bin Laden family was at the request of Condoleezza Rice, George W. Bush's National Security Advisor at that time. The Bush family has ties to the bin Ladens going back to 'W's grandfather, Adolf Bush. They've been throwing each other business for decades. Why do you think that the bin Laden family members were able to fly out of the United States on multiple aircraft after the 9-11 attacks, when no one else in the country could fly anywhere? Condoleezza couldn't resist placing Al Gore's name on the no fly list just to mess with him for awhile.

But it worked out for me. I simply negotiated with my friend, one of the underpaid, overworked IT specialists working for the bin Ladens, to move my name from the no fly list to the preferred flyers. So here I am."

"Glad you're on our side."

"It's nice to see you Amid. But why are you here?" asked Kirk.

"Harry sent me to help you guys get into trouble."

"Now that I can believe."

"When you told him how difficult it was to access the Mormon vault, he contacted me. He knew my uncle and I had dealings here."

"It seems like you have dealings everywhere. I was surprised by your contacts back in Amish territory."

"We've been trading with them for years. Nice bunch of fellows, and absolutely honest in their dealings. Anyway, tomorrow we need to go across town. There's someone I want you to meet."

Chapter 17
Resolution

That night Kirk slept restlessly.

There was a lone tree where I was standing. A jacaranda... No! A maple, oak, elm... just leafing out... young woman looking at the ground...Susan, no... someone else... a stranger looking for keys... trying to get away...the national guard started to move...someone gave the order to...march up the hill...the hill.. the guard pushed the crowd forward to the other side...they turned and marched back to the hill.. they turned all at once on command...turned and fired...the bullet screamed into her flesh, sending out jets of crimson which wrapped her body like a shroud as she turned and fell to the ground.

Kirk woke up suddenly in a sweat.

"There were no keys! She wasn't looking for keys on the ground. She was falling to the ground, dead. I couldn't help! I couldn't help!" Kirk cried out. "That's what my mind was trying to do. Make me face the truth. I stood next to a young woman and watched her die. I held her for a moment. But there was nothing I could do. So I picked up my camera and took pictures. I was so angry I wanted to document the murder of the students. Somebody had to. It all came back to me."

"It's alright baby. I'm here. I've got you." said Lucy with tears in her eyes as she held him close. "I've got you and I'll never let you go."

The Panther Chronicles Part II

Chapter 18
Sally

The next afternoon, Amid, Kirk and Lucy dispensed with the limousine and took a rental car to an isolated gated community across town. They drove slowly through the wide streets which curved along rows of meticulously maintained homes shrouded with flower gardens and lush, groomed lawnscapes. They entered a long, cobblestone driveway that curved into a loop up against a plush, modern MacMansion with a brown, stone facade. As they entered the foyer through a thick oak door capped with heavy, black metal hardware, they were immediately and warmly greeted by Randall and Nyana. The team was soon approached by a slightly overweight, tall, elderly man with a full head of bright gray hair, dressed in white slacks, white shoes, black socks and a dark navy colored classic polo shirt with an alligator logo. A black computer USB thumb drive hung from his neck by a long, gold chain. It swayed back and forth as he approached, like a pendulum on a grandfather clock ticking away the remaining years of his life. In the drive was embedded a single, small, faceted yellow diamond that matched his slightly coffee-stained teeth showing through a wide smile.

"Rufus!"

"Amid, my friend; long time no see. Your expatriates from London and India arrived a little early. We've been getting to know each other."

"Rufus, I'd like you to meet Kirk Michaels and Lucy MacDonald."

"My pleasure. Welcome to my humble abode." Rufus said as he waved his hand in a semicircle. "Let's adjourn to the pool. On a day like today it's more comfortable outside, and more private with my fountains running back there. They tend to make it difficult for anyone to hear conversations unless they're close in. I had the fountains specially tuned so the cascading water would mask out human voices. It works like a charm. It also tunes out my mother-in-law when she tries to yell at me from the house."

As Rufus led the team through the house, Kirk held back a little with Amid. "You're kidding." Kirk said quietly. "His name is really Rufus?"

"Rufus Sarduchi. It's a good Italian name. He's a good Catholic too; used to be a priest until he dropped out and married an ex nun. I've known him for a long time. He's one of my uncle's contacts in the states. He's helped in 'expediting' problems we've had with shipping goods into and out of the country."

"So much for homeland security."

The team pulled up deck chairs around a large circular table nested amidst three, tall, rock fountains that cascaded into the large curved-shaped swimming pool. A grass strip about six feet wide separated the ten foot wide, concrete pool deck from the eight foot tall cedar privacy fence surrounding the backyard on all sides. Cameras mounted on the fence scanned the house and yard. A tennis court stood off to the side. The wide bright, multi-colored fabric umbrella, growing up through the table, shaded them from the late afternoon sunlight. They were each greeted and inspected by two young golden retrievers that ultimately decided to chase a tennis ball that Rufus threw into the pool to distract them for awhile.

"Let me get this straight." said Rufus. "You guys want to boost the legendary golden tablets from the Granite Mountain Records Vault of the Mormon Church Library archives? First of all, why waste your time chasing figments of someone's imagination? And second, that place is more secure than Fort Knox. It's under ten thousand feet of solid granite. That's why they call it Granite Mountain. You'd have a better chance of stealing that Black Stone from the little square building in that mosque in Mecca. The one you sell cleaning supplies to, Amid. What's that called?"

"The Kaaba in the Masjid al Haram."

"Yeah, whatever."

"Ah, yes, I see what you mean Rufus." said Amid. "That would be stupid."

"You bet."

The Recovery Team remained silent as Rufus sized them up.

"You guys are really serious?

"We need some information. Maybe you can help us?" asked Amid.

"I owe you Amid. Those organic figs your uncle has been sending me sell like hotcakes. I package them in individual wrappers and with my markup I'm making more money than the drug runners. But I don't think the Mormons have any gold tablets. People have been asking them to produce them for years as documentation for their faith. No luck. But if you want to take a look I may be able to help. Hold on a minute."

Rufus pushed the call button on the intercom and called out. "Sally!" While he waited for a reply he asked Amid, "What kind of information do you need?"

"Building access. We thought we would sneak in at night and have a look."

"After dark? Impossible."

"Yes Rufus?" Came a reply over the intercom.

"Sally, would you come to the pool. There are some people I'd like you to meet."

"Be there in a minute." Came the reply.

"People think it's quaint that I still have an old intercom system in this big house. But you can't monitor or trace calls from it. Sometimes low tech is better, security wise."

"Wait a minute Rufus." asked Kirk. "You're an alarm expert right? Why can't we just disarm the Granite Mountain security system from outside? Bypass the code and walk in."

"Because the front door uses a simple deadbolt lock opened with a brass key. There is no security alarm, so that wouldn't present a problem. It's getting past that hail of bullets from the twenty-four hour security guards inside and outside the building that would be difficult. Once again, it's low tech, but efficient. And before you ask, they don't have a back door, fire door or accessible windows. Everything comes and goes through the front. The whole building is carved out of solid rock."

"Sounds like you checked it out already?"

"As a security expert I've checked out all the important buildings locally. Just to stay sharp, you understand."

"What do we have to look forward to as far as access to the secure stacks?"

"I'll let my young niece Sally answer that. Her parents wanted a boy and planned to name him Sal, after her old man's brother who gave them the down payment on a house. So they called her Sally. She went on to become a security expert. I taught her most of what she knows about technique, like social engineering your way past people who should know better. But the student has far exceeded the teacher. She knows all about the modern electronic crap they use nowadays. There was an unfortunate incident when she was travelling in Europe. That kind of motivated her to learn this stuff. She's been living here since her parents died not too long after that. They designated me as her guardian in their will. Here she comes now."

The patio door slid open and out sauntered a twenty something, short, thin, athletic women. Her natural blonde hair cascaded over a loose-fitting, lightweight, white, long-sleeve cotton blouse draped over tight-fitting weathered cotton denim jeans. On her feet were bright lime green plastic crocs below gold, ankle bracelets. As she approached, one could see that on her right lapel was embroidered, in green thread, the outline of a cat.

"Speaking of stacks…." Randall whispered to Kirk.

"Sally stopped about five feet from Amid. As he stood up, she smiled brightly and ran to him, giving him a strong hug, then a long, big old sloppy kiss on the lips."

"It about time you showed up!" said Sally as she gave him a gentle, affectionate slap on the cheek, feigning irritation.

"I was just looking for an excuse to come back." said Amid.

"I though I was your excuse."

"It wasn't easy for this Muslim to get back into the country. I had to pull some strings, and it took awhile. Otherwise I would have been here much sooner."

"You wouldn't have that problem if you converted to my religion; the Seven Day Opportunists." said Sally.

"I'd still look like the stereotypical middle east terrorist."

"Ohh." said Sally seductively as she pinched his belly. "You just look like my big old teddy bear."

At that the rest of the team laughed hysterically.

"Sally, you and the teddy bear can become reacquainted later on. Right now these crazy people have some security questions." said Rufus sternly.

"Oh Amid. Is this your team. The one you told me about in your cryptic messages?"

"Uhh yes. But…"

"Yes." said Lucy quickly. "Amid here is the brains of the whole team. If we ever get caught doing anything wrong. He'll stand up like the great leader that he is and assume full responsibility. Won't you Mr. teddy bear?"

"All right you guys." blushed Amid.

"How can I be of help?" asked Sally after she was properly introduced to the team members.

"We need access to the Granite Mountain Records Vault of the Mormon Church." said Kirk bluntly. "Rufus has briefed us as to the impossibility of accessing the vault. What we need from you is how it can be done."

"Well, let me give you an overview. They actually give tours of the facility. There's a snack bar, restrooms, and bookstore near the entrance. You can walk right up to the entrance of the stacks from that adjacent public area. At that point you have a problem. The outer doors of the secure area are two inch thick transparent Lexan. Those doors are open during the day, but the inner doors are made of one inch thick stainless steel bars about two feet apart. There's an electronic lock that requires biometric input along with alphanumeric codes and questionnaires."

"What type of biometric?"

"Highly advanced, both palm and iris scans."

"Questionnaires?"

"Random generated questions about the Church of Jesus Christ of Latter Day Saints. Any Mormon deepened in the faith could answer them."

"That's some pretty serious security. How do we get in? asked Amid"

"You aren't getting in while it's locked, without high explosives or thermite."

"Sally, how do you know all this?" asked Kirk.

"Well you lucked out. I was on the team that installed that system. I had a long look around inside the vault when I worked on it; just for informational purposes you understand. There's nothing there except papers and books, the history of the Mormons and master copies of two million rolls of microfilm and microfiche; nothing but records. They value their genealogy highly, so they have the original copies in an atmospherically controlled section to protect them. If you don't mind my asking, what's in the records that interests you?"

"We're not looking for records." said Kirk. "We're trying to find the fabled 'Gold Tablets' that the Mormons are supposed to have somewhere."

"There aren't any golden tablets there, just papers, books, film and a few Mormon related paintings. You're wasting your time."

"Sally, as scientists we have the innate need to explore every possibility; to examine every clue a piece at a time. As we exclude each possibility, what is left, however improbable, must lead us to the truth." said Randall. "The tablets may not be there, probably aren't. But we need to confirm that, and if they're not there we're hoping we can find a clue as to their location."

"Very well. I'll help if I can. But you owe me dinner and a move, Amid."

"You mean dinner and a movie?"

"You heard me the first time. We have to make up for lost time."

"Jeez. Can we focus?" asked Randall. "So it's impossible to break in after they close for the day. Even if we could, we would also have to work our way through a whole series of sensors in each room on our way to the closed stacks. So how do we get around the alarm system?"

"Can we do something low tech like enter the public area and remain after hours? Maybe hide in the janitors closet or restrooms?" asked Lucy.

"That's a good thought. Sometimes simple actions can override elaborate systems. But they sweep the area before locking the main doors." said Sally.

"What about the internal sensors?" asked Amid.

"They're all standard, industrial strength infrared. But they're on a swivel mount for calibrating them to the room." said Sally.

"How do we get around them?" asked Kirk.

"When we're in the library during the day, can we push up the sensors outside the secured stacks to face high. Then we can walk around without activating them?" asked Amid.

"They inspect the sensors before closing. It's on their daily check list." said Rufus. "These guys are thorough. They don't just do security theater like those fools at the airports."

"How do you know this?" asked Lucy.

"Because Sally wrote the checklists." Replied Rufus. "She made the system tight. We really didn't plan to break into the Vault. You know what I mean. So she didn't leave a 'back door' in the security system."

"And what about the alarms in the closed stacks?" asked Lucy?

"That's a problem. I've got an idea how to solve it. How about a relatively low tech solution here, guys?" asked Nayana. "If we can set free some mice into the secure stacks, the librarian will freak and immediately call an extermination service. Librarians fear mice more than anything. They have a tendency to destroy important documents rapidly. I know how hyper I get when I see a mouse around my work area, since I often have ancient paper documents on my desk. We stop everything until we're free of them."

"Mice might migrate out to the snack bar. There's not much to eat in the main vault." said Amid. "We need to make sure they're worried specifically about the secure area. How's this? I can make up a number of infrared micro-laser emitters that I'll place in the room just outside the closed stacks, the day before we want to enter. I'll aim them into the stacks. Since the outer wall there is transparent, the emitters will produce warm spots in the vault even with the doors locked. They'll be timed to emit at random intervals during the nights. That will simulate a mice infestation to the infrared detectors. I'll spread some fresh mice scat and spray a little mice urine around. I can toss that through the bars during the day when the outer doors are open. Security will think that mice are activating the sensors and will call us to eliminate them. I might even toss a dead mouse into the vault just to heighten the effect."

"But they could call any exterminator." said Lucy.

"While we've been talking I logged into the online yellow pages. There's only one exterminator in town." replied Amid. "I can jack into the phone system of that exterminator. When the Mormons call, we'll answer. Rufus and company can supply a duplicate exterminator van, equipment, and coveralls. We enter the vault, spray it with some noxious stuff to keep everyone out, and we look around for awhile with small metal detectors tuned to respond to gold."

"What about the security cameras in the vault."

"They'll capture images of us looking around, presumably for vermin. They won't be able to identify us later because we'll have masks on to protect us from the spray; no fingerprints because we'll wear gloves. Also, nothing will be missing. If we find the gold tablets they won't be able to report them as missing will they?"

"No. But they'll come after us fast."

"Come after who?" asked Rufus. "I don't even know who you guys are. I'm just doing a favor for my young friend Amid."

"Rufus." said Amid. "I guarantee you are better off not knowing everything."

"Amid", said Kirk. "I don't even want to know how you're going to get mouse urine. But I like the infrared transmitter idea."

Chapter 19
Staging

The next morning Amid went on a visitors tour of the Granite Mountain records Vault. He setup the infrared micro-transmitters in the public visitors area just outside the closed stacks, magnetically attaching them to the metal shelves amidst some old books and pointing them into the vault. He surreptitiously blew some mice scat past the bars and into the vault while the outer Lexan doors were open, using a straw from a soda he bought earlier at the snack bar. He dispensed with the mouse urine idea, because of logistics problems.

The team spent most of the day in the hotel suite meticulously planning the event. Randall, Kirk, Sally and Rufus used temporary hair dye to alter their appearance. Kirk and Lucy took a break and visited the Mormon Tabernacle at Temple Square. Nyana continued to work on her translation of the Walum Olum. Randall disguised the small, handheld gold detectors to resemble the vermin odor sniffers used by exterminator companies. Amid used his electronics prowess to sidetrack the phone system of the only exterminator company in town. He setup a remote bypass which he routed to the hotel so he could monitor all calls to the real company. Rufus and Sally prepared a duplicate exterminator van, and clothing, and the team waited for the call.

That night the infrared transmitters caused warm spots to appear in the vault, setting off the sensitive infrared detection alarms. The records vault director was awakened at home several times by the alarm company. After the director went to the vault and let the security people inside, they found nothing unusual. The next morning the director and head librarian searched the vault while a security expert checked the alarm system. The head librarian shrieked as she discovered the bane of libraries; mice turds lying about. After the security people confirmed that the timing of the alarms might indicate that they were set off by rodents, the director and head librarian decided to take definitive action. They immediately called the exterminator.

"Heads up everyone." said Amid. "The phone's ringing... Good morning, Mountain Meadows exterminating. How may we help you? Yes. Yes... Oh that's terrible. We'll reschedule our other customers. Of course your vault takes precedence. Those mice can do a lot of damage in a short time. We'll be there soon. Goodbye."

"Round up the troops."

"Amid. How long were you in the prison in Teheran?" asked Sally as they walked together. "You didn't go into detail the last time I saw you."

"I got there the day before Kirk arrived. And I was only there for a week after he was released. Kirk described the conditions in the prison to Harry Stratford, a friend of our family. Harry recognized me from Kirk's description and bribed me out. Harry rescued me once before when I was a child. He took care of me then, hiding me from my family's enemies until he located my uncle In the port of Jeddah in Saudi Arabia and could safely move me there. Kirk saved my life. Not only by his report to Harry, but also his perverted sense of humor while in the prison. If you can laugh in a situation like that, it gives you strength to go on."

"What were you doing in Iran?"

"My uncle wanted to establish some trade relations with the Iranians, rugs, fabrics and artwork. The Iranians like tourists, including those from western countries. They have no inherent objection to Saudis also, even though we are of different Islamic sects. One reason is that the holy places are in Arabia and the Shia Iranians want to maintain decent relations with the Sunni Saudis so they can go on pilgrimage there. But there are those in Iran who try to instill fear into the hearts of the gullible, to maintain control. So they create enemies from whom they will protect us, if we surrender our freedom to them. They are the old guard, mostly old men who are slowly losing control of the younger generation. Kirk's idea of a trigger, that I told you about, may have worked if it had played out a little differently. I don't think it will take much to initiate a rapid change there.

Abd al Aziz Fahd Ahmad Haqtuii directed the death of my parents. Haqtuii is...was a Saudi. He was in Iran engaged in nefarious trading activities with the Iranians. I suspect arms trading. He was doing his Iranian contacts a favor by training the police how to be treacherous. My parents were mistakenly thought to have converted to Christianity, so Haqtuii led a raid on our home. He recognized me and had me imprisoned. He was also responsible for killing Susan, Kirk's old flame."

"You said he *was* a Saudi?"

"He's dead now. He drowned in the Arabian desert. It's a long story. Remind me to tell you about it sometime."

Chapter 20
Connections

L ucy and Kirk had taken the tour of the Mormon Tabernacle at
Temple Square. As they started to walk out, Lucy asked the
docent if she could remain for awhile. The docent had no objection.
Kirk took a seat in the front center row of seats facing the organ, to get
a proper overall compositional view in preparation for taking a
panoramic angle stitched photograph of the interior.

Lucy walked up in front of the great organ where the acoustics were
at their best, turned towards Kirk, and began to sing:

Come away with me, in the night
Come away with me
And I will write you a song ......

She continued with all the lyrics.

"Norah Jones" she said. "Do you like it."

Upon hearing Lucy sing, Kirk was moved by her vocal ability. He
felt as if a new connection had been made between them.

"What Kirk? Why are you looking at me that way?"

"I had no idea that you sang so well. That was beautiful...it touched
my heart."

The remark caught Lucy off guard. Even though he was
affectionate, Kirk was not usually so open, so unguarded, so poetic. It
seemed at that moment that Kirk was free of the baggage that had held
him down, free to give entirely of himself to another.

"I, I don't know what to say." She said as she walked down the
stairs toward Kirk. "I just felt like singing to you; never had a chance
before. My mother taught me to sing. She was a professional singer in
Arabia until she was ostracized for marrying a westerner. The chamber
was open so I thought I'd see how I sounded here. I imagined what it
would be like standing up there in front of that great organ, wearing a
blue robe and singing with the choir. I sang in a choir in high school
and college."

"Zahrah, there's something I've been wanting to say for some time." Kirk said as he reached out and took Lucy's hands in his. "When we're together I feel...that is, that we were meant to be. I uh.., I love you. I think that we should...that is...will you..."

"What's up guys?" Randall interrupted as he and Nyana walked forcefully into the theater.

"Oh, Oh, did we interrupt something?" Nyana asked apologetically when she noticed Kirk and Lucy holding hands and looking intently into each others eyes.

"That's all right." Lucy sighed. "Kirk and I were just...talking."

"Well if you're done talking we have work to do. We got the call." Randall said coarsely. "Let's find the artifact and blow this place."

As they walked away hand-in-hand, Lucy stopped, turned toward Kirk, smiled, and said, "Yes."

Chapter 21
Action

The Recovery Team headed for the Granite Mountain Records Vault.

"Remember." Kirk said. "That vault room is full of paperwork and film. We're looking for something out of place, such as a metal container or safe, or a film container of a different shape or color. Look for some area that has extra security measures. We'll deal with those as we encounter them. We'll have Sally, and a bunch of tools, with us, so we should be able to circumvent most problems.

Soon the team arrived at Granite Mountain.

"Lucy, and Nyana will be outside the vault in the snack bar and atrium with communicators, mixing in with the tourists. If anything unusual goes down, they'll let us know." said Amid. "Let them walk in first so we don't appear to be together."

After a few minutes, Rufus, Randall, Amid, Sally and Kirk entered the building and presented their card to the guard behind the information desk as another guard off to the side looked on. He made a phone call to the librarian. While they waited they looked around and acknowledged the presence of Lucy in the gift shop off to the side and of Nyana, who was slowly walking around the perimeter of the circular atrium, looking at the paintings depicting Mormon History. The librarian arrived shortly.

"Welcome." she said warmly. "I'm Mrs. Thompson. Thank you for your timely response. We seem to have a small infestation of mice. How they could have possibly gotten in here is beyond me. We had some mice gain access shortly after the construction of the vault, before we modified the air intake system to exclude critters. That solved the problem for years. I never expected to see them again. Mice can do a great deal of damage. They're a librarian's bane. We've had you out periodically to run checks. But you've never found any."

"Yes but you never know when varmints are going to show up." Randall responded with a smile and a nod to his colleagues. Under the circumstances we thought a quick response would be appropriate."

"As a matter of fact, I checked the records just before you arrived and your firm made a quick inspection just four days ago. I wasn't here at the time. Didn't you find anything then?"

Randall, Kirk and Sally looked at each other in surprise.

Rufus quickly responded. "Oh yeah. That was me." He admitted as the others looked on in amazement. "I was doing a quick walk through to see what equipment and people we would need so I could stage out for our more thorough upcoming regular inspection. We were surprised to hear from you now. Well. We should get on with it."

The others glared at Rufus. His face seemed to turn a slight shade of red as he looked away and Mrs. Thompson headed for the vault.

The librarian put her palm onto the biometric sensor at the vault entrance as she looked into an iris scanner resembling binoculars. The red LED light turned green. She then typed in a seven digit code. A series of questions came up on the small liquid crystal display which the librarian answered quickly. No one on the team could see what was on the screen because of the low viewing angle, adjusted that way for security purposes. Seconds later the solenoids activated five, one inch thick, solid stainless steel deadbolts set into the door at equal intervals from top to bottom. She grabbed the large handle and pulled open the vault door, motioning our team inside.

"I'll leave you to your work." she said. I'll be in my office. If you need anything, let one of the guards know and he'll fetch me."

Mrs. Thompson walked back to the guard/information kiosk and spoke to him briefly. She then walked away, headed back to her office. The guard motioned for one of the other guards who was observing the action. The guard behind the desk spoke in a low voice to the other guard, who then took up a position about ten feet in front of the vault door, and facing away from it. His orders were to keep everyone else away from the vault while the team worked inside.

The team slid into their white, hooded, Tyvek, Hazard suits. They pulled on their full-face air purifying respirators and nitrile examination gloves. This provided them with full coverage so they couldn't be identified by the continuous digital video recordings made by the cameras inside the vault. Even their shoes were covered by the booties built into the Tyvek suits. There were no cameras outside the vault because the continuous presence of armed guards was thought to make them unnecessary.

The team entered the vault and walked around with their gold detectors, pretending to use them as electronic sniffers to ferret out mice. They set several mouse traps along the floor perimeter as they looked around. Each team member searched a sector of the vault for an index to the vault records. They them met back near the vault entrance. Here they were far enough away from the guard so he wouldn't hear their conversation.

"Any luck anybody?" asked Kirk quietly.

"Nothing." Replied Randall, Sally and Rufus almost in unison.

"There must be an electronic index." said Kirk. "Did anyone see a computer terminal?"

"Negative." each responded.

"Anything unusual or out of the ordinary?" Kirk asked with an air of hope.

"Nothing, nope, nada." they responded in turn.

"Wait a minute. Look at that painting. It's Joseph Smith right?" asked Randall as he pointed to a wall behind a nearby shelf. "At least it looks like him from the pictures I saw during our research."

"Yes. And look closely at what he's holding. Gold tablets?... no, they're wooden tablets."

"See that security camera. All the other ones are on movable mounts. That's the only one that is on a fixed mount, pointed to the Smith painting." said Sally.

"Let's check it out. Sally you're on." said Rufus as he looked around the shelving at the guard to make sure he was still looking away. "I'll spray a mist in front of that camera. They'll just think we were spraying for mice. That'll give you five minutes before it clears up. Ready?.. Set, go."

Sally quickly removed the painting from the wall, revealing a small safe. She recognized the manufacturer, and setup a powerful microphone listening unit. Then she accessed her personal database of safe operating systems on her iPad. Using the data, and her extensive knowledge and experience, she opening the safe in about a minute.

"That safe wasn't a particularly secure unit. I guess they didn't expect anyone to get through their other security measures. Let's see what's inside."

"Four minutes."

"Copy this quickly." She said to Randall with a sense of urgency as she handed him a small, old book with a weathered, brown leather cover. "I need to put it back soon."

Randall photographed all fifty pages of the book in record time with a miniature high speed digital camera while Sally pulled out a metal box and handed it to Rufus. Rufus quickly opened it and gasped.

"Well I'll be damned. We didn't find the gold tablets but will you look at this. Aren't these the wooden tablets you guys were talking about."

Inside the metal box was what appeared to be the wooden copy of the gold tablets. They were small, each about the size of a pocket notebook; about a quarter of an inch thick and made of compacted Birch bark. The small tablets were secured together at one top corner by a finely woven, but strong, string, possibly made of animal gut. They appeared to be coated with some kind of oil as a preservative. Rufus handed it to Randall without saying a word. Randall finished copying the diary and photographed the nineteen wooden tablets, front and back.

"One minute."

Randall quickly handed the wooden tablets to Sally who placed them back into the metal box. She then placed them and the book back into the safe and closed the door, replacing the painting over the safe just as the mist started to clear. Everyone had moved away from the area and finished setting mouse traps. Randall did another quick visual scan of the vault just in case they missed something.

Everyone moved out of the secure stacks and the team left the building, signaling the lookouts, who followed shortly thereafter. Later they all met back at the hotel.

Before leaving, Rufus spoke with the librarian.

"We fumigated the whole area. We used a fogger that won't hurt the paperwork or films back there at all. It's completely safe except for mice. Have the janitor throw out the traps in two days and call us back if there are any mice present. I think we solved your problem."

"What is the cost?" asked the librarian.

"You've been such good neighbors to us that I'm not going to charge you for this call. It's on the house. We'll have our regular inspection crew schedule an appointment in the near future."

"Well thank you so much." she replied. "Isn't that such a nice man." she told her assistant as Rufus headed for the door.

Chapter 22
Review

Back at the residence.

"Okay Rufus. Come clean." demanded Sally. "What's with that 'previous inspection' of the vault?"

After a slight pause...

"I ahh... got a call from a former client. A Mr. Sanders. He uh... asked me to check out the Mormon vault. He said some oddballs, if you'll excuse the expression, might be headed this way. He wanted to know what you were after. He didn't mention any names. Then you guys showed up."

"Why didn't you tell us?"

"You didn't ask."

"C'mon Rufus." said Sally sternly. "You were just trying to squeeze out a few bucks by playing the field. Aren't these guys paying you enough."

"Heh! I didn't know what was going on when he called. When I figured it out, I decided to play along with him for awhile."

"Rufus. We need to know what he knows." said Amid.

"He said he had some guys looking into what you were doing at Snake Mound."

"Serpent Mound." said Lucy.

"Yeah, Serpent Mound in Ohio. He keeps an eye on it for some reason. He didn't say why. He said his guys were probably just trying to extend their contract. Anyhow they continued to monitor your movements. They found out you bought tickets to Salt Lake City. That made him curious. Then he called me. We had some 'business' dealings a few years ago. I never met him. He just sends a bank check."

"Who's he work for?" asked Sally.

"What makes you think I would know?"

"Give me a break. I've been living here for years. You check out everyone. You probably had a dossier on the team here before we hit the vault."

"Sally, you know me too well. I'm sorry, I'm just an old snoop. It's in my genes. And it kept me out of trouble. Okay. He works for some dude by the name of Penn. He comes from an old Pennsylvania family. Hey wait a minute. I wonder if he's descended from old William Penn, the founder."

"You think." said Randall.

"His ancestors stole the land from the Lenape Nation." said Kirk.

"I'll brief you later Sally." said Amid.

"And I'll 'debrief' you later." Sally whispered into Amid's ear.

"So old man Penn is still looking for something." remarked Randall. "Maybe he believes in the existence of the gold tablets too."

"Or he's just covering his ass." said Rufus. "People like that are always suspicious."

"Look who's talking." said Sally.

"Rufus, Sally, we couldn't have done it without you." said Amid.

"Our pleasure," said Sally. "It was fun. I'm not exactly sure why we did it, but it was fun. It brought back the old days. See you again tonight? Amid" she asked demurely as she handed him her cell phone number.

"I'll explain it in detail to you later Sal." said Rufus as they were leaving. "Try not to get into too much trouble guys. Adios."

"That's a nice set of resources." said Amid as he and the team walked to the car.

"Don't be such a letch, Amid." said Randall in jest.

"Hey. I was referring to Sally's technical prowess. She would make a nice addition to the team. You see that cat embroidered on her blouse? That's her occupation...cat burglar. Not only is she an expert in alarm systems, but she's an expert gymnast and climber."

"And she has such nice posture." added Kirk with a smile. "Where did you meet her?"

"Actually, I bought her."

"What?"

"It's a bit of a story. I'll tell you all about later."

Chapter 23
Eureka

The Next Day. Back in the hotel room.

"Okay, let's review. First question: How did the Mormons get the wooden tablets? That was a surprise."

"Ward, then Rafinesque had access to them." said Lucy. "The Mormon's must have somehow acquired them from Rafinesque's estate. Remember, Mormon's are preeminent experts at tracing geneology. They probably traced Rafinesque's relatives until they found one with a bunch of old wooden tablets with scribbling on them. They could have bought them for a song."

"Nyana, can you translate the Walum Olum from the photos of the wooden tablets." asked Kirk.

"That will get me started. I'll be able to make some assumptions to refine my translation algorithm. But there is no way to establish the authenticity of the wooden tablets, even if we had them. The original text is on the gold tablets. The Mormon's know that. That's why they didn't go public with the wooden tablets; that and the fact that they can't translate them. I took a look at the photos, and it's going to be difficult for me to translate."

"Here it is." Randall said as he brought up the photos onto the 40" LCD television. "That book in the vault is the personal diary of Joseph Smith. Look at this. Smith said that after he found the gold tablets he spoke about them to a number of people in the area. He speculated that word got back to the Lenape and they 'liberated' the tablets from Smith. That's why Smith said that an angel told him he could no longer have access to them. He was covering his 'access' so to speak. The other entries pretty much cover Smith's later life."

"Then we might logically conclude that the Lenape took them along as they were displaced westward by the tyranny of William Penn's son. They temporarily buried them, or stored them in one of the small caves for protection, at Serpent Mound as we initially surmised. Then they moved farther west and took the tablets with them. They could be anywhere." said Lucy.

"They must have lost them along the way. The Lenape today are scattered all over the Midwest." said Kirk.

"I believe that assumption is warranted." said Nyana.

"Yeah. If they had the tablets, the Lenape would have showed them to the world a long time ago to establish their ancestral claims to the Eastern lands and to secure their tribal status. Unless...what if they lost the tablets at the Serpent Mound, and Putnam found them?" asked Randall.

"Putnam spent three years excavating there." said Lucy. "He would have publicized the find to prove his work wasn't in vain."

"Not if he didn't know what he found." replied Randall.

All together the team exclaimed. "The clay tablet!!"

"I'm guessing that the tablets are in the Peabody Museum of Archaeology and Ethnology at Harvard University in Boston." said Nyana. "They're stored with the Serpent Mound artifacts collected by Frederick Ward Putnam. He didn't miss them in his excavations. He simply didn't recognize them. The gold tablets might be hidden inside of that clay tablet. I've seen such tablets used in other excavations to conceal valuables."

"That makes sense." said Kirk. "Susan's research turned up evidence that there were a number of deaths among the Lenape when they lived at Serpent Mound, especially among the elders. They would have been the ones in charge of hiding the tablets. There might have been only one or two people involved, and they died before revealing the location to someone else in the tribe."

"Yes, it makes sense from a psychological perspective also." Lucy agreed. "The Serpent Mound was sacred. When migrating peoples settle on sacred ground, especially the elderly, there is sometimes a desire to die there. They feel closer to the spirit land. That's why there were burial mounds associated with the main mounds built all over the country."

"What a bad deal." said Randall. If the Lenape hadn't lost the tablets, they wouldn't have lost their lands. The tablets would have proven their claim."

"No, not at that time." said Kirk. "Remember, William Penn's son and other greedy individuals falsified the claims to Lenape Lands.

Also, the doctrine of manifest destiny, propounded in the mid eighteen hundreds, encouraged white settlers to advance toward the Pacific Ocean. Native Americans never had a chance against the forces of greed and racism. However, if we can recover the tablets, we may be able to do some good now."

Chapter 24
Sally Redux

That evening as the team sat around a table at poolside.

"Okay Amid", said Lucy. "Tell us about Sally."

"Well Sally was always restless. As a teenager she talked her parents into allowing her to travel with a group of friends on a backpacking trip around Europe. Like most kids, she lacked sound judgment. One evening in Spain, she and some of her friends accepted an invitation to a beach party from a nice looking, well dressed and very polite young man. It turned out he was a shill for a white slavery ring. Sally went to the party and ended up being drugged.

She woke up at a secret auction house at the port of Jeddah, where my uncle has his offices. I had been working there with him for years after Harry rescued me from prison. My friends had been urging me to go to a local out of the way auction to see some of the exotic goods up for bid. None of us knew that on the day we arrived that kidnapped women and children would be offered up as goods for slavery. I'm surprised the old man in charge there let us in. He said that he thought we should learn the ways of the world. Of course, he threatened to track us down and kill us if we told anyone what went on there.

There is where I first saw Sally. A young woman about my own age, standing in the shadows behind the stage, just a short distance from where we stood. I watched as they ordered her up the steps. She complied without protest, actually smiling as she ascended. She appeared under no restraint. They had her dressed in classic British schoolgirl attire; Blue blazer over white blouse, knee length tartan pleated skirt, and white socks under polished leather black shoes. I guess that's what turns on those wealthy Arab perverts who buy and sell humans. I found out later she had been drugged by her captors. Fortunately she hadn't been abused. Those Arabians like their slave women 'pure'.

My friends and I were disgusted by the whole affair. But we forced ourselves to smile meekly as the old man escorted us out and invited us back when we had enough money to bid. I asked what would become of the 'items'. He responded that most would go home tonight to their new owners, but the 'British schoolgirls' would be held here tonight, where their new owners would try to sell them at a profit to some rich businessmen coming in from Russia tomorrow.

I returned home that night and related the story to my uncle. He said it was about time I knew about some more of the sordid happenings in the world. The death of my parents and my time in prison seemed like more distant events compared to imagining the horror of the life of slavery for this young woman. This was here and now, and it hit me hard. I asked my uncle what we could do.

"What we can do." he said. "Is to mind our own business. These men are heartless vultures and don't play by any rules. We don't want their kind of trouble coming down on us."

After giving the situation some thought, I asked. "What if we buy her? That way it's a business transaction and they won't bother us. They'll have their money."

"Great idea my smart nephew." he responded. "But where are you going to get the money? These young women don't sell cheaply."

I looked him in the eyes without blinking, staring at him without uttering a word. After a minute he blinked, then smiled. I knew I had him.

"You little shit. What time is the auction tomorrow? And by the way, you're going to have to work overtime to pay me back."

Next day I attended the auction. My uncle came with me but sent me up front with bidding instructions and said he would catch up to me later. After a time the slaves came up for bid. I saw Sally standing there, looking much like she did the night before. Except, she had a very visible red rash on her arms and neck. The other women were auctioned quickly and fetched high prices. I was worried that my uncle would withdraw his support when he saw the apparent cost of my little escapade. I didn't have to worry. Somehow word circulated that Sally was used merchandise and had a sexually transmitted disease. By the time she came up for bid, most of the men had left. I acquired her for a fraction of what I was expecting to pay.

In addition to being an excellent merchant, my uncle is also a professional herbalist. He buys and sells them often, making a tidy profit. That night after we returned home with Sally, my uncle pulled a small container from his pocket and set it on the mantel.

I asked him about it, and he told me not to touch it. As he winked at me, he said it can cause a terrible rash that can take days to clear up.

It turns out Sally had been drugged by her captors to keep her compliant. It took several days to clean it out of her system. She was ecstatic when she knew she was safe with us and we would get her home safely.

Because of her kidnapping, over the years Sally learned all she could about electronic security systems and locks. She said if she had had some knowledge during her transit to Arabia, she could have escaped her kidnappers. She also studies martial arts so nobody can easily mess with her again."

"Wow… That's quite a story Amid. You did good." said Lucy as she hugged him.

"Now if you'll excuse me, I have a hot date." said Amid.

The next day the Recovery Team headed for Boston.

Chapter 25
Karl Schmidt

I *wonder if Harry told Kirk I'm tracking him?* thought Karl.

Karl Schmidt had been shadowing the team under orders from Harry Stratford. Kirk's new satellite communicator was low-jacked with an experimental GPS tracking device. It pulsed Kirk's location at random intervals to a receiver built into Karl's digital universal time programmable Casio watch. Instead of listing the time by standard cities such as Rome, New York and London as Karl pushed the zones button, the display read 'London, Paris, *Kirk*, New York'. From any wireless internet access point Karl could not only track Kirk & company's current location, but also his previous path.

Amid was using the Stratford Group company credit card to pay expenses for the team. This allowed Karl to also access all charges through Harry's company account to provide more detailed tracking. When Amid charged airline tickets to Boston for the team, Karl headed from Ohio to Boston Logan Airport.

Chapter 26
The Psycho-Path

"So your feeling better?" asked Dr. Smith.

"Absolutely." replied Kirk. "My last dream freed me. My mind just wouldn't let me face the truth. The woman I stood next to at Kent was killed. I didn't want her to die, and I felt guilty for taking pictures."

"I'm the expert Kirk. Let me do the interpretations."

"So how do you explain it. Dr."

"The same way you did. Your explanation seems correct. Always keep in mind that you're a photographer Kirk. Keep shooting. And don't worry about feeling guilty. Of course there is nothing you could have done; at Kent State University, Jackson State University or in Iran. But since you're a real person, a mensch, you will always feel like you might have done something. The time to start worrying about yourself is when you stop feeling guilty. Check back with me once in awhile. And keep Lucy near."

Chapter 27
Logan's Run

Up to now Karl had been following the team's progress from a distance. His instincts from years of counterintelligence work told him to move in closer. They had proven correct. When the team arrived at General Edward Lawrence Logan International Airport, they were immediately followed by two sleazy-looking characters. Karl's suspicions were aroused when the two individuals moved quickly out of sight as the team proceeded through the airport.

The two sat at a distance just outside of the secured area, but within sight, as the team recovered their luggage at the carousel. When the two pulled out a laptop computer, Karl immediately opened a small case and pulled out an XO learning system computer that he purchased from the One Laptop Per Child Project. It was the only computer on the market that had a built-in wireless dual antenna strong enough for his purposes. Karl quickly booted it up and accessed an 'activity' that the Stratford Group had created called 'Keymon'. This allowed him to monitor the keystrokes of any computer within twenty meters using the mesh network capabilities unique to the XO.

The two sent an e-mail message saying that they had the team under close surveillance.

Karl waited for the right opportunity to act. He needed to delay the two thugs.

The luggage handlers took some time to unload from the Salt Lake flight. As one of the two characters went to the bathroom, Karl inched closer and pretended to drop his magazine near the laptop case, which was under the seat next to the other man. As Karl leaned over he quickly sprayed the case with a low yield contact explosive, a trick he learned from listening to Randall Thomas's childhood school days' exploits. Karl quickly moved out of the area so none of the team members would spot him.

The team finally recovered their luggage and left the airport. The two thugs followed quickly, but as they neared the exit the man with the computer case accidentally bumped a portly woman and the contact explosive was set off. This let out a loud retort and produced a small puff of smoke. Although the smoke quickly dissipated, the woman screamed, bringing security running to the scene. Karl walked by and photographed the two with his cell phone as he exited the airport. The two thugs were held for questioning while security sorted out the melee.

Chapter 28
Ivy League

"We don't usually allow access to the storage area. But your credentials are impeccable, and I'm suitably impressed by your analysis of Mughal epigraphic texts, Dr. Murthy." said Sarah Jones, the young museum director who Nyana had contacted en route to Boston. "I read several of your translations. As an incurable romantic I was particularly interested in your work about Shah Jahan, his wife Mumtaz Mahal and the Taj Mahal. What a romantic story."

"Please, call me Nyana. I think every woman in the world would like such a monument of her husband's love. But remember she died giving birth to her fourteenth child; not too romantic after all.

These are my research associates, Dr. Randall Thomas, Lucy Graham and Kirk Michaels of the London Museum Geophysical Institute, and Amid al Rahid of the Stratford Group."

"Pleased to see you. Mr. Rahid, I'm glad we had a chance to meet. Now I can put a face behind the voice on the telephone. I can't thank you enough for arranging that very large donation to our museum from the Stratford Group."

"My pleasure."

"I hope we have a chance to have dinner later?" asked Sarah.

"I would love to; but perhaps another time. Our team is on a tight schedule this time around."

"I'm a bit surprised that a museum director in Boston would have knowledge of Indian epigraphic translations." said Randall.

"Oh Randall, don't be so provincial." said Nyana. "We museum people are charged with disseminating our knowledge as far as possible. Most of our operational grant funding requires it. With the internet it's easy to access even the most obscure material. For example, I was familiar with your 'Serpent Mound' in Ohio even before you mentioned it when we were in London. And besides, this is Boston, it's not off the beaten path; it is the beaten path.

Also, you might be surprised to know that the most accurate slides and the most detailed studies of the Ajanta caves we visited in India are in the India collection at the University of Chicago."

"You're kidding." replied Randall.

"Not at all. Researchers from around the world worked together, uniting the planet in a knowledge network, long before the internet. That simply made it much easier.

Now Sarah, let's have a look at Mr. Putnam's contribution to our knowledge base."

The group walked twenty feet down a long gray, concrete block corridor about six feet wide, with a brown-tiled floor. Sarah unlocked a gray metal door, reached around the side and flipped a switch. A bank of old, heavy-looking, metal, fluorescent lights, hanging from the ceiling by chains, slowly came to life. As dust tumbled from the lights, for an instant it gave the room the look of an ancient tomb that had just been violated by impertinent explorers. Sarah escorted the group into this large room. Ceiling height metal shelves stood at attention, arranged into six rows. Each row was labeled clearly at the end of the shelf as to the specific collection it held. The last section against the far wall was labeled 'Putnam, Fredrick Ward'.

"Here's the Putnam collection." Sarah said as she pointed to a series of drawers sitting on the lower shelves. "I'm afraid it's pretty boring; just a lot of flint arrowheads, necklace disks and spear points, and a clay tablet. But enjoy. I'll be in the office if you need anything. There's a box of nitrile gloves on the counter if you want to handle anything."

The team opened the cabinets one-by-one, looking intently at the artifacts for any useful information. Then they came to the drawer with a clay tablet resting on foam padding. Nyana carefully removed the tablet from its nest.

"The lettering on the clay artifact translates as, 'The tablets are here.'" Putnam thought it meant they were at Serpent Mound, and gave up when he couldn't find them. He thought the clay tablet was a simple marker, a cover stone. But 'here' meant literally here, inside the clay 'marker'. The Lenape buried them at Serpent Mound when they recovered them from Joseph Smith. Since the Lenape were worried that someone else might find them, they disguised them this time. They encased the gold tablets in a clay box. Because of the weight it appeared to be a solid clay object. Then for some reason the Lenape misplaced them.

Your hypothesis is most probably correct; that the natives who hid them perished before they could reveal the location to anyone else. Putnam later removed the clay tablet. That's why we couldn't find it there."

"We can't break open the clay tablet, so we'll have to have it x-rayed." said Kirk.

"But I just photographed the clay cover tablet, preserving the inscription, and the tablet itself really has no particular significance. It was just used to hide the gold tablets, like putting the Hope Diamond in a cardboard box." said Randall. And if we tell the museum staff, they'll spend years arguing about how to analyze it. Plus we need to get a look at it before the Lenape find out and demand that we return it immediately under the "Native American Graves Protection and Repatriation Act of 1990. Then we would never be able to analyze the tablets."

"Either that or the Mormons will try to 'acquire' them." said Randall. And they have some significant resources. There may also be others with an interest.

"But we can't just cut the clay off. That might break it." said Kirk.

"I have an idea how to solve the problem," said Nyana. "Hand it to me and I'll show you."

Kirk reluctantly handed Nyana the tablet, curious as to her solution to their cunundrum.

"Oops!" exclaimed Nyana as she dropped the clay marker onto the concrete floor, careful to have it hit on the edge. "My bad."

The tablet split just as Nyana had anticipated, showing two sections and a small fragment.

"I thought you were into preserving antiquities, Nyana." Kirk exclaimed.

"Kirk, the clay covering material is of little historical importance in this case. The cardboard box analogy is accurate. Plus, in my years of research I've seen many objects of value hidden in clay boxes. I found this is the best technique for opening them. Now let's see what we have." she said as she bent down to recover the artifact.

"Well look at this!" Nyana exclaimed with delight as she picked up the clay tablet and pried it open wider until it came apart and exposed its inner secret. She reverently revealed the object inside. Nyana put on some thin white cotton gloves she brought with her and removed the artifact.

The team members were ecstatic. Here before them was the object of their quest. The sacred gold tablets inscribed by a holy person, detailing the Great Prehistoric Migration of the Lenape ancestors. A lost record, recovered from antiquity, and now in the hands of the Discovery Team. The tablets were very thin, but definitely not just gold leaf, as in the Greek graves. These were meant for continuing use, like a journal. There were nineteen sheets, connected at the top left corner by a silver-colored wire to which were attached a series of small artifacts.

"Let me take a closer look at those?" asked Randall as he reached for the nitrile gloves.

"Don't even think about it." said Nyana. "Cotton fabric gloves only in a controlled laboratory. Besides, here comes the director."

"Time to go." said Kirk.

The Team reassembled the clay cover box and placed it back into the drawer with the other Putnam materials. Nyana quickly slipped the tablets into a passport holder hidden under her blouse, along with the small fragment of the clay tablet that had broken off. She removed her gloves and placed them into her pocket.

"Thank you for your help." Nyana told Sarah. "There's nothing of interest to us back there." she said truthfully as they walked out.

"Ms. Jones." said Amid quickly so as to distract her. "I'll be returning to London soon, but with your permission I'll arrange for the Stratford Group to sponsor a short sabbatical for you to England, say a month or so, if you can get away. That way you can tell us all about your programs here at the museum, and you'll have a chance to meet Mr. Stratford."

"That would be wonderful. I'm sure I can get away. But please call me Sarah."

"Only if you call me Amid. Goodbye, for now Sarah." He said as he gently shook her hand.

After they left the building Randall couldn't resist saying, *"Only if you call me Amid.* I don't think I've ever seen anyone hit on a woman as fast as you did Amid. You're collecting them right and left. "

"Don't forget, Randall." said Nyana. "You hit on me as soon as you saw me."

"I can't help it. You're irresistible, my little Indian princess."

"A month in London eh Amid?" said Lucy. "That's pretty romantic. Mr. Kirk Michaels here takes me to a cheese factory in Ohio and buys me a piece of apple pie. Then he thinks he's going to get lucky."

"Hey! Wait a minute." said Kirk.

"All right heathen brothers; and sisters. I meant it as a professional invitation. My uncle encouraged me to make contacts wherever I go. Besides, you met Sally. She'd have me renditioned to Somalia if she caught me messing around. We've been communicating regularly. But I think we're going to start spending more time together. If you guys don't get me into more trouble."

"Amid?" When did you arrange for that contribution to the Peabody Museum?"

"While we were in Salt Lake City, as soon as I knew we were headed here, right after Nyana contacted the director. I figured it would smooth over our visit, act as a rationale for our being here, and deflect questions. A little social engineering, just like the visit to London."

"Well it worked. Good thinking. And you may have started an interesting, 'professional' relationship."

"Yes. That director was cute." said Kirk.

"Okay you guys."

Chapter 29
Thuggery

The two thugs at Logan airport finally convinced airport security that there had been a misunderstanding and that they were harmless. After questioning several nearby vehicle rental agents, and bribing the critical one, they were able to determine the make, model and license number of the van rented by the team. The agent also helped to locate the van since all their rental vehicles were equipped with GPS monitors. Location- Harvard University. The thugs rented a Bronco and caught up with the team just as they were leaving the University.

The Panther Chronicles Part II

Chapter 30
Highway robbery

The trip back to Ohio in the van was exhilarating, as each member of the team took turns inspecting the treasure.

They stopped for lunch at a choke and puke in Medusa, Pennsylvania. They then continued along the Ohio turnpike toward Cleveland with Nyana at the wheel. On an isolated stretch of highway a white Ford Bronco pulled up slowly next to them on the left as if it were passing. It seemed to match their speed when it was parallel to the van. Nyana looked over and saw two strange men looking over at the team. The Ford stayed even with them even as Nyana varied the speed of the van. She alerted the team and they agreed; they were being followed.

The passenger in the Ford rolled down the window, pointed a gun at Nyana, and ordered her to pull over. Her racing instincts took over as she decelerated and pulled over behind the Ford so suddenly that the aggressor didn't have a chance to react.

"Hold onto your butts." Randall immediately said. "Nya takes no prisoners."

The Ford driver hesitated, then slowed rapidly, trying to stop the van. Nyana anticipated this action and instantly moved over to catch the Ford on the right rear bumper. She then accelerated, spinning the Ford around ninety degrees and pushing it into the wide, grass-covered median strip. The Ford flipped over onto it's top, slid down the median and spun around again. Kirk looked through the rear window and could see the doors fall open on each side and two men roll out onto the grass. They stood up and staggered to the side, while brushing the dust off and giving the team the one fingered salute.

"Glad you were driving hon." said Randall.

"I took advantage of the fact that those Broncos are flippy." said Nyana.

"I wonder if those turkeys figured out we recovered the tablets." asked Lucy. "Amid. Did you mention that to Sally?"

"Negative. I told her we thought they were in the vault at Granite Mountain. Besides, we had other things to talk about."

"Wait a minute." said Randall. "Did we talk about them at that last rest stop? They were probably listening then. I thought that one guy was pointing his iPod at us as we sat at the picnic table. But it didn't make sense at the time. They wouldn't have messed with us there with so many people around. They waited for that stretch of open highway."

"Relax." said Kirk. "We talked, or rather we listened to you talk about the advances in ground penetrating radar, remember. But from now on everybody on the alert."

Karl had been following at a distance. He was pleased to see his help was no longer needed. The team was aware of problems and would not be taken off guard again. Karl exited and headed for Cleveland.

Chapter 31
Analysis

The team met at Kent State University Carlson Science Center Laboratory, in the Liquid Crystal Institute.

"How long do we have, Kirk?" asked Lucy.

"My friend Tony said we could use this, the physics and the chemistry labs all weekend. Classes are out until Monday. The lab's been cleaned, so even the janitor won't be here. Tony is the only one doing research over this weekend. He said he'd stop by later to see if we need anything. His friend Ralph lives in the chemistry lab and can help us."

"What have you got, Nyana?" asked Kirk.

"The first section of the tablets is in a very formal mode of Ancient Greek." Nyana said. "It translates clearly as: '*All must say. 'I am the child of Earth and Starry Heaven...*' That's the same as on Greek Orphic gold foil burial tablets of the fifth century B.C. that I saw from Crete. Those are the instructions for the initial greeting to the stewards of the rivers in the afterlife. The inscription later continues in first person singular: '*I am sent as a light, to guide mankind*'."

"Sounds familiar." said Kirk

"The remainder of the tablet is the Walum Olum Pictographs. It's going to take a little time to translate that. But I've been developing a specialized computer algorithm based on the Brinton reproductions. That will help me to achieve a high level of accuracy with the pictographs. It's based on my previous work with some difficult epigraphic translations I made in Sanskrit. I've adjusted the model based on the known accuracies in the Walum Olum and the material in the Holographic chamber from the Panther Chamber. It's self-correcting; the more I translate, the more accurate it becomes. It will then go back and make corrections in the work on a real-time basis. I'm also working on a three-dimensional rendition. A new idea that might prove rewarding."

"Your so smart, you should have been a fox." Randall said.

"I am a fox. And don't forget it."

"Alright guys, let's focus a little. Lucy, will you and Randall work up the physical characteristics with the scanning electron microprobe while I setup my lighting to photograph the tablets in High resolution." Kirk said. "Nyana, I assume you're alright working off the initial digital photos?"

"That's fine Kirk. For the time being. I'll do a high quality three dimensional imaging scan tomorrow morning, with Randall's holographic camera."

Six hours later the team met in the Science Center Lounge.

"O.K. Lucy, what have you go so far?" asked Kirk.

"The individual tablets callipered out at a thickness of 2mm. The letters and pictographs are tiny shallow engravings, but very legible with ten power magnification and apparently quite durable. That's how they were able to get so much information on nineteen small tablets. They resemble the laser engraving you had Apple Corp. inscribe on the back of that iPod you bought for me, Kirk."

"What did it say Lucy?" asked Nyana.

"If music be the food of love, play on."

"Oh, how sweet. I didn't know you were such a romantic, Kirk." said Nyana. Why can't you be like that Randall?"

"Because I'm in the middle of a scientific project that could change the history of the United States." said Randall rather impatiently.

"What else Lucy?" asked Kirk.

"Well you can see how lightly the iPod is engraved, but likely to last a long time. Same for the tablets. You can see how small everything is. That might explain why Joseph Smith reputedly used a special 'crystal' to aid in the translation. He was using a simple magnifying glass most probably made of polished quartz that he sometimes carried to look at rocks and leaves. I had a magnifying glass as a child and looked at everything. I think most kids played with one."

"What type of engraving tool did the scribe use ?" asked Randall.

"Astonishingly. There are no tool marks visible, even at very high magnification. Even laser light engravings like those on the iPod show irregular markings. The lettering and pictographs on the gold tablets weren't really engraved; the markings just appeared as a distortion in the matrix. They are smooth down to the atomic level. Nyana looked at the photomicrographs from the scanning electron microscope, and she concurs."

"The tablets all measure 85mm by 52.53mm. This is the 'golden ratio' or phi, 1.618, named after the Greek sculptor, Phidias, who used the ratio in his sculptures. It's also known as the 'divine proportion'. Other artists throughout the ages have also used it because it's very pleasing to the eye. That's how I recognized it, from my studies in proportion and perspective." said Lucy.

"Hold on." said Amid as he pulled an object from his wallet and held it up to the tablets. "They're exactly the same size as my credit cards."

"That's right." said Lucy. "One of the first things we learned in applied art class is to make a product visually pleasing. Apparently the credit card art consultants now apply the same techniques as the divine scribe who created the gold tablets."

"Interesting. What's the composition?" asked Kirk.

We analyzed it using an electron microprobe and our noses." said Randall.

"Excuse me." remarked Kirk with surprise.

"Some of the most accurate scientific instruments are the human senses. And researchers today often use their noses for initial analysis, despite the fact that their laboratories are loaded with the latest and greatest equipment. We gently heated one of the tablets and readily detected the scent of copper. The microprobe confirmed that and detected for gold and traces of platinum in the matrix. The metal is an alloy; gold, silver and copper, as we speculated." said Randall. "It's equivalent to about sixteen karat gold. Any more gold and it becomes too soft; any more copper and electrolysis destroys it over time. The tablets were apparently vapor gilded to atomic thinness to reduce that possibility even further. It's a pretty advanced process. Whoever made them knew what they were doing.

"What's the silver wire in the corners that held the plates together?"

"Mithril. That's why it's so strong." Lucy replied with a poker face.

"What?"

"Just kidding." she laughed. "No hobbits or dwarfs were involved. It's really a platinum-based alloy, very strong. Imagine that, a platinum alloy that's well over ten thousand years old. The oldest report of the use of platinum we've previously had was by the Egyptians, over three thousand years ago.

We're using several methods to try to date the beads in the necklace. Randall can explain the techniques in detail to you better than I."

"Maybe later, or we'll be here for hours." said Nyana.

"That's great guys, good work. How soon on those bead results?" asked Kirk.

"Tomorrow afternoon, if we continue early in the morning.

"There's a nice inn here in Kent that I booked us in for the night." said Amid. "If we finish, we can catch a flight out of Akron/Canton airport tomorrow."

"What airline, Amid?" asked Randall.

"Stratford Air. Harry agrees with your plan to return it to its rightful owners, but he wants to take a look at it first. You know how excited he gets with this stuff. He'll meet us at the airport, have a look at it and then send it on to the prescribed location. He has everything arranged already for the return of the tablets to the rightful owners."

"We all agree that his plan has the most merit and will be most effective.' said Kirk. "Although it's going to cause an uproar."

"Well." said Randall. "Uproars are our specialty."

The team headed for the nearby University Inn.

Chapter 32
Synthesis

The next day the team continued to work on the artifact. They assembled their data in the late afternoon.

Let's examine all the evidence a piece at a time, so we can be absolutely sure of what we have." said Kirk.

"Very well." said Randall.

"First: The clay box was never opened after the Lenapi sealed it before burying it at Serpent Mound. It remained in the undisturbed collection of artifacts retrieved by Putnam. They used a cement like material to seal the box, rather than a kiln to fire it closed, which would have destroyed the tablets. This box helped to protect and preserve the tablets. Interestingly, the clay box matrix and cement are both composed of a serpentine asbestos type material which acted to make it fire resistant and at the same time reinforce it with the asbestos fibers. That had to have been brought in from outside since there are no serpentine rocks like that in Ohio. The material origin is possibly the metamorphics from the Adirondack Mountains in Western New York state. We'll confirm that soon. I took a sample over to the geology lab for X-ray analysis. The new computer system makes for a fast analysis.

Second: The clay of the box itself was fired prior to the insertion of the tablets. When a rock is heated to that extent, it records the ambient geomagnetic field. Comparing that to the orientation of fired materials of known age, from other nearby investigations, we can date it. The process is not extremely accurate, but it gives us a timeframe. Based on the geomagnetic orientation of the fired particles in the matrix, the clay box is approximately two hundred and fifty years old. Remember, magnetic north moves fairly rapidly. That's why you have to set the magnetic declination on your compass every few years so your reading of true north is accurate. We confirmed this timeframe with thermoluminescent dating. Randall got those results back from Crazy Ralph in the Chemistry Lab. It's a good thing I saved a piece of the clay box.

"Wait a minute." said Kirk. "I thought that technique only worked with materials in place, in situ, like stuff found in fire pits, because you had to know their compass orientation, where they were found."

"That's how they used to do it." replied Randall. "But when there is an irregular firing or heating, such as is the case in this piece of the tablet, some of the magnetic particles in the clay matrix don't have a chance to reorient themselves, thus giving us a comparison between the two particles. The angle tells us how old it is because we know how long it took the earth's magnetic north to shift by that many degrees. It's still approximate, but a good way to get a minimum age.

"I thought it took much longer to perform that type of analysis." said Nyana.

"Normally it does, because it used to require significant preparation." said Randall. " But I showed Ralph a new technique the Arts People at the British Museum are using. I helped them to refine it based on my years of geophysical research. The method is much faster. Ralph is in hog heaven now."

"I thought the Arts People ran you out last time you were in their labs." asked Kirk.

"Not after I explained the whole story of the Black Stone to them. They thought the entire affair was cool. Plus, I let them use my lab equipment. Were good buddies now."

"Third:" continued Lucy. "As I mentioned yesterday, the wire that held the tablets together at the corners had large beads attached, made from zircon, obsidian and pieces of mammoth teeth. We hit the trifecta. We dated the zircon with fission track dating, electron spin resonance on the mammoth teeth and hydration dating on the obsidian. That securely established the date of the wire attachment and thus the minimum age of the tablets at over ten thousand years."

"Wait a minute." said Kirk. "Obsidian is volcanic glass. The structure is unstable since it forms rapidly from fast cooling lava. Doesn't it try to stabilize by devitrifying, or crystallizing over time? That would mess up any chance of hydration dating."

"It does devitrify." said Randall. "But it takes much longer, typically millions of years. So our procedure works here. Each of those methods are ideally suited to the type of material being analyzed. It's kind of spooky though. It's as if we were, at this time, supposed to be able to confirm the date of the tablets. We couldn't have done it just a few years ago. Kent has a very advanced lab."

"Then it appears these are the genuine article. A piece of history unraveled." said Kirk.

"Nyana. Did you have a chance to get your high resolution holographic images?"

"You bet. The holographic camera has a macro feature that allowed me to get in close to the pictographs; great resolution. I already fed the information into my computer application. It's cooking the data now."

"Great job everyone. Speaking of cooking. We need to get moving. Let's clean up and get out of here." said Kirk.

Just after they packed up and were ready to leave, the door was thrust open and two figures appeared. The men in the Ford had tracked them to the Liquid Crystal laboratory at Kent.

"Nobody move!" They shouted in unison.

"So you're the tough broad that blew us off the highway." He said to Nyana. "Nice driving. But now, we're in charge." He said as he pointed his gun in the direction of the team. "Get whatever they have." He told the other man.

"I'll take all your cell phones." He said as he waved his gun at the team. "Nobody calls anyone."

The second man looked around but only saw standard laboratory equipment. The gold tablets were temporarily stashed in a desk drawer in an office off the lab. He spotted the Pelican case containing the ground penetrating radar, sitting in the corner. Assuming it contained something important, he picked it up and rejoined his partner, as the team slid their cell phones toward the man with the gun.

The gunman retrieved Kirk's phone and looked at it carefully as he turned it.

"This is a strange thing." He said very quietly, almost in a whisper.

Thinking quickly, Kirk asked loudly. "What did you say?"

"I said, ASSHOLE." He yelled out. "THIS IS...ARRGH."

The gunman fell instantly to the floor and shook violently for several seconds, just before he passed out cold.

"Taking his cue from Kirk's question. Amid and Randall were already on the second man, pinning him to the ground.

"What just happened?" asked Nyana.

"Kirk's new satellite phone." said Amid. "A hundred thousand volts of pure knockdown. The strangers voice activated the shock circuit since the device didn't recognize it as Kirk's."

"A bug zapper. Can I get one?' asked Nyana.

"You're on the list sweetie." Responded Randall. "Kirk got the first one because he was on the move."

"I don't know who you guys are. But you've been harassing us for nothing. We're just researchers testing some new equipment." said Lucy to the conscious miscreant as she opened the Pelikan case and showed it to him.

"Have a look at this case. This is a state of the art ground penetrating Radar unit. Nobody knows about it yet. That's why we've been so secretive. But it goes on sale after we turn in our report confirming how well it works. Why are you so interested in it?" she said as she pointed Kirk's phone at him.

"Keep that thing away from me." he sputtered. "Were just collecting some information for a client." He said nervously. "I don't know who he is. We just receive instructions and after a job our bank accounts get bigger. We never met anyone face to face. Why were you guys in Boston?"

"As if it's any of your business! We partnered with them on the Radar test."

"Smile guys." said Randall.

"What the hell are you doing?"

"I just took your pictures for our files. I hope you don't mind. If you ever come near us again they'll end up on the internet on every sex offender registry in the world. Understand?"

"Hey, we're cool man. Can we have our guns back?"

"Tie them up and we'll have Tony turn them over to the campus police." Kirk said quietly to Amid. "He can say he caught them snooping around the lab. That ought to keep them out of our hair for awhile."

"What about the guns?" asked Amid.

"Take them over to the Art department and fire them in a kiln. If the police find guns on these turds they'll want to investigate further. We don't want the campus cops to think too much."

Chapter 33
Lucy

Early the next day the team prepared to leave.

"Why are we bugging out so early Kirk?' asked Randall.

"There's just one more stop we need to make before we head back to London. It's only a few miles from here."

"What's that?" asked Lucy.

"A surprise. You'll see."

Kirk drove down highway 59 then followed route 8 north to the Steels Corners Road Exit. As they headed west into the Cuyahoga Valley National Park the scenery morphed from a noisy asphalt and concrete interchange into a lush green surround. The parking lot was mostly empty in the morning as the next performance in the outdoor theater wasn't scheduled until the evening. As they walked along the curved path from the parking, they followed the music from the practicing orchestra to the amphitheater.

As they turned a corner, Lucy recognized a familiar figure and ran to greet him. Her father James MacDonald had flown in from London after Kirk called.

Lucy turned to Kirk and asked. "Okay, what's going on?"

"I hope you don't mind my being so presumptuous. But, you looked so happy singing at the temple in Salt Lake City...well, I thought you might like the acoustics here at Blossom. I often came here while I attended Kent State. So I contacted your father for his opinion. He thought it was a great idea to rent the facility here as a surprise for you. I hope you don't mind. Will you sing for us; for those of us who love you so much?"

"Of course." Lucy said as she threw herself around Kirk and gave him a big kiss of gratitude. Then she hugged her father again, then headed for the stage.

Everyone else took their seats at the back just under the curved spaceship-like architecture of the canopy, where the acoustics were the best.

"What's she going to sing?" Nyana asked Kirk.

Before he could respond, James answered, "I setup the orchestra and secured the center here on Kirk's request while you were all finishing your analysis of the artifact. Then I remembered Lucy's favorite song from her childhood. She sang it often while she played in the garden and didn't know we were watching.

"Isn't that the Cleveland Symphony Orchestra in the pit." asked Randall.

"It is." said Kirk. "They're playing in concert tonight here. So we hired them for a time to back up Lucy.

"Who's paying for all this?"

"Well." said Amid. "You see, Harry Stratford made a rather large donation to Blossom Music Center. We'll let Harry know about it later, when he's in a good mood and has recovered from the shock of our other recent expenses. Besides, Harry has too much money and I feel obligated to relieve him of his burden.." said Amid.

"...so he will become a more spiritual person." Everyone said in unison again.

"Say guys." Remarked Nyana as they waited for Lucy to prepare. "The serpent mound is interesting, but in my research I noticed there's another mound here in Ohio that's called the 'Alligator mound'. But it appears some researchers think that it might represent a panther rather than an alligator. Some of the older drawings, before it was damaged, look more like a cat. Now if we could find a bird mound that looked like a condor, we might speculate that the mound builders are related somehow to the Inca tribes of Peru and Bolivia, since those three animals represent the Inca culture."

"You mean the people who built Machu Piccu in Peru?" replied Randall.

"Yes. And other terraces and related structures in that area of South America."

"We should look into that sometime.", said Kirk.

The musicians started to play. Lucy recognized the melody after the first three notes, and with a smile on her face she stepped forward to the microphone stand and made a height adjustment. She looked out at her friends and colleagues and nodded to them.

Then she glanced upward and then bowed her head slightly as she whispered to herself, "This is for you, mother." Her heart aglow, Lucy began to sing a Persian ballad that her mother sang to her as a child, as she tucked her in for the night.

Chapter 34
Surprise

"Did you hear from Laurel and Hardy yet." Asked Mr. Penn of Mr. Sanders?

"I did. They said they were delayed for awhile in Kent, Ohio, and couldn't get through to me. Some trouble with a satellite phone."

"I didn't think those bozos could use a satellite phone."

"Apparently not. But they finally called on a land line. They said the people of interest were just scientists testing some new ground penetrating radar equipment and didn't want anyone to know about it until it was on the market. They thought our dolts were involved in industrial espionage, trying to jump the patent or something."

"So they got their tits in a ringer again. See if next time we need a job done you can find some operatives who are a little more competent."

"Will do."

"What were these... 'scientists' doing in Salt Lake City?"

"My contact there, a guy by the name of Rufus, said they were Mormons on pilgrimage to the temple and library. And he trades with the Arab kid's company."

"Then we have nothing to worry about. I didn't think we did, but I wanted to be sure. I don't like surprises."

Chapter 35
Justice

The Recovery Team was back in their haunts at the private library in their quarters at the British Museum.

"Well, the Lenni-Lenape are ecstatic." said Lucy. "Did you see the news headlines on CNN. It's been on all day. They say that apparently someone found the lost gold tablets that the Mormons laid claim to, with proof that they were stolen from the Lenape. The United Nations Institute for Indigenous Peoples received them anonymously with a modern, documented, accurate translation and comprehensive physical and optical analyses attached. Copies were also distributed simultaneously to all of the news agencies throughout the planet. This confirms the Lenape's prior claims to large areas of Eastern North America.

The government lawyers are already circling the wagons. The ultra-conservative Penn Foundation will be leaking dollars too. Old man Penn won't be buying off as many politicians anymore. It looks like the Lenape will be receiving significant compensation for the sins of William Penn Jr. and others who appropriated their land. And more importantly, it permanently secures their recognition as an independent tribal entity, something they've been seeking for many years and only partially achieved to date. They plan to place The Gold tablets into the National Museum of the American Indian at the Mall in Washington, D.C., for all to see.

"Nyana, did you have enough time with the tablets?" asked Kirk.

"Yes. You see I couldn't tell much from the worn epigraphs in our holographic reproduction of the Panther Chamber. But the pictures from the wooden copy helped move me farther along. When I took a look at the original Gold Tablets, I was able to see the pictographs very clearly. It was then that I realized that William Penn was right when he referred to the Ancient Lenape language as a kind of shorthand, he said, "*one word serveth the place of three, and the rest are supplied by the understanding of the hearer.*" That clued me in.

I fed the holographic images from the original tablet into my program. It raised each two dimensional character straight up, then displayed them as three dimensional representations in the form of a cube. Only then could it rotate and translate accurately the three figures on each of three axes represented by the six sides. It's essentially compressed information. Randall helped a lot with the algorithm adjustments due to his study of x-ray crystallography as an undergraduate. In that field you deal in three dimensions and multiple axes with mineral crystals.

Having a multidisciplinary team is a great help.

You see, the Lenape ancestors thought in three dimensions. That's the only way they could have survived at a subsistence level, especially on an epic journey. Predators can come at you from any direction. The same applies when hunting game.

Their holy scribe compressed this historic journey into two dimensional pictographs to save space; for the same reason we compress computer data now."

"Then somehow she knew that in the future some good looking fox would figure it out." said Randall.

"Wait a minute." said Kirk. "Are you saying the Walum Olum is written in a three dimensional language? A synthetic language. That seems almost impossible."

"That's why appropriate characters and pictographs were borrowed from multiple languages, and many original ones created." replied Nyana. "They had to make sense from three dimensions. It's extraordinarily difficult to create such a language. I would have needed a supercomputer and ten years to do it. I feel like a child who just learned her A,B,C's. It's a humbling experience. This opens up a whole new world. We epigraphers are going to have to go back and apply this technique to everything we've discovered in terms of language since the inception of our field. We'll have to reevaluate our hundreds of years of knowledge translation and transfer. Clearly a superior intelligence was at work here."

"How were you able to do it so quickly?" asked Lucy.

"I adapted modern computer archival compression software to my translation program." continued Nyana. I had to, in effect, 'Unzip' the pictographs and then translate them using both archaic and modern forms of the Lenape language.

The 'Lenape Stone' aided in the translation. It acted as a partial Rosetta Stone. No one could do that in the past without high speed computers and the use of my algorithm, the one I spent many years developing. As the result, many mistakes were made in the other translations of the Walum Olum over the years. They failed to factor in the three dimensionality of the pictographs. Thus they only obtained partially information, despite their best efforts, and induced many inaccuracies. But the most glaring error was the direction of the initial great migration."

"How's that?" asked Kirk.

"Conventional Lenape history has their ancestors migrating out of the West to the Eastern Seaboard, then south from Labrador. But this was a secondary migration. They've been here a long time. They were returning home to their eastern lands at that stage, from their exploration of western areas. They didn't enter from Asia, from the west to the east across a Bering Sea land bridge as many thought. They came from the Mediterranean area landing at what is now...New York. That's why the Walum Olum had some characteristics of a language predating Greek, and containing similarities to pre-Egyptian Hieroglyphics. They migrated across the Atlantic Ocean at the end of the last ice age, forced out of their island home by some catastrophe, and guided by a great teacher, a tall lady of the light."

Epilog

And they sailed their boats across the partially frozen ocean, culling food from the wildlife that drifted into their path, and the fish in the sea, miraculously providing manna. At length the birds appeared. Finally, they saw land to the west. They arrived on a peninsula in the harbor, later to become a small island as the land ice melted and the sea rose. Here they gave thanks to the great Manito, at the precise spot where another tall lady would come to stand many summers from now. And she would also pray:

"Give me your tired, your poor,
Your huddled masses yearning to breathe free,
The wretched refuse of your teeming shore.
Send these, the homeless, tempest-tossed, to me:
I lift my lamp beside the golden door." [1]

END

1 Emma Lazarus, "The New Colossus"